# HARBOR SEVEN

Thoughts on the journey from a man well traveled.

To order additional copies: www.harborseven.com

For information on bulk orders:
Harbor Ministries
P.O. Box 21984
Lincoln, NE 68542
info@theharbor.cc

**TO THE JOURNEY.**

# CONTENTS

# GRATITUDE

To my wife Marcia, whose life story should have pointed her away from God, but who has taken steps toward Him no matter what life has thrown her way. Her relentless heart for God and her enduring love for people is a constant inspiration. Our almost 25 years together have been filled with fun, laughter, struggle, challenge, forgiveness, love, hope and excitement. I'm excited for the years ahead.

To Drew, Ali and Dylan, whose stories and lives have been the inspiration for this work. If I accomplish nothing more than just being your dad, it would be worth it.

To Cindy Conger, Pat Williams, Ali Schwanke and Sharon Sevenker. Without their creativity, attention to detail and encouragement, I never would have finished this book.

To Ben Harms, who has helped give this story a face. His creative talents and unique gift mix helped make this come to life.

To the first group of RHYTHMinTWENTY participants. They took a chance on the crazy vision and dream of Harbor Ministries and entered a three-year journey that is changing all our lives.

To my parents, Lloyd and Zella. The way they lived their lives helped keep me in a restless and relentless pursuit of something bigger. They lived life with rhythm and always seemed to keep the end in mind. My dad left us 25 years ago, but his life continues to inspire many to this day.

Here's to the hope of finding a rhythm to our lives, to leaving a legacy, to finishing well.

THE INVITATION

So, I am sitting on my favorite rock at the Alluvial Fan in Rocky Mountain National Park, and I am struggling. This place has been a place of restoration, refuge, clarity and celebration over these last couple of years.

We just launched our fourth group of RHYTHMinTWENTY with 20 leaders; leaders from all over the country who are embarking on a dangerous journey of pursuing God, listening and taking steps that are changing everything.

A few years ago, who would have thought that God would use these events, and the successes and failures of my life to help launch Harbor Ministries? Who could have guessed that at some of my lowest moments that insights, clarity and inspiration would come?

As I thought again about publishing this book, some fear, and a ton of doubt set in. It's humbling to put a project like this out. Do I really believe there is value in my ordinary story? Are there lessons, truth and insights from my journey that could really help others?

But, as I listened to the stories of others this week, I was reminded that there is great value in all of our stories. There are many moments in all of our lives that can encourage and inspire others to take needed steps in their journeys. For me, it has been critical to slow down, unplug, seek some solitude and really listen. Listen to what God has been saying through my life. When I have done this over the last few years, dangerous things have happened.

That is easier said than done. Recently it took a major winter storm to force me into a needed change of pace, and the quiet mornings gave me space to reflect on the previous months. In that forced but desperately needed quiet, God reminded me of the unique and sometimes difficult ways He had broken through and revealed Himself to me during what had been a very treacherous couple of years. And He reminded me that there are parts of my story that others need to hear.

If not for the quiet, if not for a season where I stepped off the treadmill and was forced to look at some things, I would have been in real trouble.

I was reminded today that it was in the quiet on another mountain, above Quito, Ecuador, that God began to renew the dream of investing in strategic leaders. He stirred awake longings to launch a ministry that would deeply invest in 20 emerging leaders at a time. He fueled the hope that if we could come alongside just 20 leaders a year and share with them the importance of times of solitude and quiet, deep connections and inspire them to start and finish well, we could change the world.

There is no doubt that a dangerous vision, a dangerous hope, dangerous steps of faith, dangerous contentment and deep peace can be birthed in you as well. But, for that to happen, much will be required of you. If you are willing to truly risk, and to chase God with everything you have, then you will be dangerous to an enemy as well. You will stand a much better chance of living with rhythm and staying the course in your faith, at work and with your family. You will be ready to step into whatever God has in store for you and you will be much better equipped to finish well.

As you read this book, and explore some of the ordinary events of my life, I would encourage you to read slowly and be fully present with the struggles and questions that you will see. I hope that you will take some time to reflect, listen, seek refuge and hear the voice of God in your own life. I hope you will find a needed harbor, a place of deep connection that will help give you the centeredness and strength you need for the weeks, months and years ahead.

It was December 22, 1986, and I was looking forward to an adventure with my dad. In three days we would set out to go deep-sea fishing, then to a college bowl game and eventually join the rest of the family on a Caribbean cruise. Through the years, my parents intentionally exposed us to new places and new experiences. As a result, I was taught to see life as an adventure. I learned that life could be more than a monotonous routine to merely survive; it could be risky, surprising, spontaneous, and at times a whole lot of fun.

I could hardly wait for the newest adventure to unfold, but life detoured our plans and sent me on a very different journey.

Alone.

My dad, the person I counted on for quiet direction, a stable foundation, an encouraging word and much-needed wisdom, suddenly dropped dead from a heart attack.

It was over.

Everything shifted. All the questions that seemed so easy to answer were not so easy anymore. The churchy conversations and the easy, pat answers were simply not enough. I felt lost. I had no map. This was new and treacherous terrain and the guy who had provided direction was gone.

Grief took me to a place I'd never been before and I started to pursue God in a raw, honest, and sometimes risky way. It was up to me to wrestle with the difficult questions of life and faith. Finding direction was now my job. I not only had to find that direction for myself, but to somehow help guide others and maybe even leave a legacy like my dad had for me.

My dad just missed meeting our first child, Drew, by a few months. Though he would not be there to coach me through fatherhood, he had instilled in me a deep desire to invest in my kids. Before they were born I made the commitment to be there for the big moments in their lives. I determined to try my best to provide stability, a sense of direction and purpose, and to hopefully point them toward a passionate pursuit of Jesus. I chose to live out my values as best I could. Most every day of his life, my dad demonstrated the values he held close. Through his quiet walks with God, his practical jokes, his love for family, his uncanny ability to make life fun and to see the best in every situation, I caught daily glimpses into what he valued most.

I determined to give it my best shot and to do my best to pass on his passion for life, that sense of rhythm, that foundation, that he had so quietly, yet extraordinarily demonstrated.

On our infamous family vacations, I remember my dad being notorious for making spontaneous decisions. He always started with a map and a plan, but he would avoid asking for directions and often choose instead to just see where the road would take us. We quickly learned that vacations, and life itself, should be experienced to the fullest extent possible. Yet even in the middle of our wildest adventures, we knew the map was in the glove compartment and could point us back to the main road if the signs, the landmarks or our own misdirection took us too far off course.

That map gave us freedom to go off the beaten path, to explore, and to discover our own path.

In essence, that is what this book is about. Our natural navigation system, though capable of getting us from Point A to Point B, can end up skewed in all sorts of directions. What we perceive to be the correct path may actually lead us far off the map. We all need a map and we all need the wisdom and experience of other people to navigate the peaks and valleys of life.

Each one of us will come to a point in our journey where we must honestly wrestle with who God is. We will need to put away some of the perceptions and beliefs about God that this culture and others have put on us and passionately seek Him out, then decide if we can truly follow Him. Each of us was created with unique talents, personal experiences and amazing stories. Hearing and remembering God's singular whisper to each of our hearts, will help point us to the destinations that are part of this crazy journey.

Even as a boy, I sensed that I was destined for something more. I would wander back to the pasture behind our house, climb the small hill to lie in the grass and imagine doing great things. Even then, I knew that I wanted to make my life count.

I wanted to be Luke Skywalker. In the original "Star Wars" movie, Luke stares at the horizon with the two suns, dreaming of what he could see and where he could go. He was yearning for an adventure; for a mission. I remember thinking, "I want to do that!" I craved the adventure and the discoveries. I wanted a chance to have radical impact. I desperately wanted to be part of a bigger story.

I still want the same things today.

I don't want to let those dreams slip through my fingers.

I need to hold them close to remind myself that God does speak and He has revealed Himself to me. Remembering gives me direction when I encounter setbacks and disappointments; it gets me back on track when I screw up. I need to relish the moments when I stand on a mountaintop with God, celebrating the successes and the adventure. Remembering helps me endure the times when I wander in the wilderness.

I don't want life to quench my spirit and cause me to lose heart.

Over the years, I often told my kids about King Josiah. The Old Testament tells the story of this boy who became king when he was only eight years old. The Bible says there was no greater king than King Josiah. How is that possible? How could someone so young be such a great leader from the ages of eight to 30?

I believe it was because he led from his heart.

As a young person, life and disappointments had not yet squelched his vibrant heart. With the idealism, passion and honesty of youth, he led a country and impacted an entire generation.

Impacting generations is something I take very seriously. Even though my father died when I was only in my 20s, it was then that I realized how much he helped me navigate life. I ached for his guidance and direction and I still do. He wasn't a man of many words, but when he did speak, his words were weighty. They made a difference. There was just something about him that called me to something bigger.

Many things promise to guide us and many things say they can fulfill us. I have tried to find life in a lot of different ways. Sometimes that search has been exciting and fun. Other times it has led to disappointment, indifference and pain. So it is not empty words when I say that I have found that an authentic relationship with Jesus is the only thing that brings the depth and meaning we long for. At the same time, we do not exist in a vacuum; we need other people to walk beside us and encourage us along the way.

Listen for the people in your life who are calling you to something more.

And determine not to travel alone.

I offer the pages of this book as a guide and I invite you to join me as we meander through the deserts, shout from the mountaintops and hang out in the valleys. As you read the pages ahead, I realize that many of you have a life story that is far different from the one outlined in this book. Perhaps you've lacked people to help you navigate the twists and turns of life. Some of you may have experienced deep disappointments, abandonment, rejection or things far worse.

And many of you, like myself have had to just be survivors; we have had to figure parts of it out on our own.

It is my hope that this short trip together will help fill that void. In my relentless search for meaning and purpose, in my deep desire to live a life of rhythm and balance, in my heart's longing to leave a legacy, through the highs and lows, the mistakes and heartaches, I have discovered a few truths from my journey. I have stumbled upon things that have helped point the way when the path was not so clear. I hope the pages ahead will help provide direction for your journey, that God's wisdom will be exemplified in these words and phrases, and that you will be challenged and encouraged to take the next step.

I guess I'm asking you to allow me to be your guide and to use this book as your roadmap.

I can't promise a smooth ride, simple formulas or seven steps to anything, but that's okay. Some of the most fantastic places on earth can't be viewed without going off the beaten path and climbing a few mountains.

STOP ONE  -  FIND THE RHYTHM

# FIND THE RHYTHM

*Finding rhythm and balance is not fighting against the current and it's not an acrobatic act performed on a tight rope, but a long, slow walk.*

It was hot and still. The clouds came quickly from the west. It was an ambush, the kind of storm that stirred up fear in the hearts of people on the plains for generations. For five minutes, the sky threw hail toward the ground like it was releasing an intense fit of rage. When the storm finally retreated, tens of thousands of dollars worth of corn was strewn about and shredded in the muddy fields of our farm, pulverized by the massive hailstorm.

Forty-five minutes later, my dad drove up the driveway in his olive green Ford pickup. Despite the devastating loss, he retained his sense of humor and calm demeanor, unchanging in his interactions with my mom and me.

Later that evening, I watched as he took a long, slow walk around the perimeter of his fields, which had been ruined by the hailstorm. Years later, one of his best friends told me that my dad was working things out with God while he was on that walk. He told God that if He wanted His tithe, He was going to have to come and get it because it was lying in the field. I will never forget the image of my father taking in the loss and surveying his wasted fields. I will never forget what it looks like when a balanced man has a bad day.

I didn't often see my dad sitting down with a Bible or reading a book. He rarely gave us lectures. Instead, he lived out what was important to him. He didn't try to put on a show—he just kept his words and actions very consistent. On the day the hail came, his circumstances changed dramatically, particularly his financial standing. However, his focus and priorities remained steadfast. Years of an ongoing conversation with God had readied him for moments like this. On a day-to-day basis, he balanced his emotions, his energy, his time and his priorities. In many ways, he was ready for a day like this. It hurt, but it didn't knock him totally off balance.

Luke 2:52 says, "And Jesus grew in wisdom and stature, and in favor with God and men." It is clear to me that Jesus developed strength and depth in His life by developing and finding a sense of rhythm to His life that would sustain Him in the difficult times that were to come. There are many things that can knock you off center and, sooner or later, you will feel the effects of being off-kilter. For me, the list of things that have, at times, knocked me off balance is extensive: the death of parents, bad choices, struggles with sin, loss of friends, financial pressures, career choices, etc. The list is likely to get pretty lengthy for anyone of us. If we don't have a sense of what it takes to keep things in balance when life happens and we take some hits, sooner or later we find ourselves in trouble. Without a sense of balance and rhythm, we are at risk to be taken out or, at best, left ineffective.

We are all familiar with the stories. A young married 20-something, filled with passion and potential, notorious for taking risks, running 100 mph, but not taking care of his own world. His life was way out of whack and, as a result, he was left vulnerable and his spiritual life became empty and superficial. It was the "doing," not the substance of who he was, that became important.

A 30-something father of two, whose whole world became the adrenalin of work and the next sale. He had a neglected wife, a stale walk with God, and a lack of people in his life who asked him the hard and challenging questions, opening the door to poor decisions that will deeply hurt and impact him and his family for years.

A 40-something ministry or business leader who was widely affirmed by many for leading a "successful" and growing organization. But the years of service, the pressures of point-leading, the loss of accountability from those close to him, undealt-with disappointment in God and boredom in his faith have led to a lonely walk of leadership. The roles of leadership at work, family, business and ministry made it hard to be real with his struggles, questions and doubts. The lack of rhythm in his life set him up as a target and put him in jeopardy of finishing well.

## A Balancing Act

Oftentimes, when I hear people talk about what it takes to be balanced, it simply wears me out. The illustrations of spinning plates and juggling balls, trying to keep one foot firmly planted and evenly balanced on the high wire makes me very tense and tired. Something is wrong with this picture. So what is it? What does it really mean to live a "balanced life"? Balance is not achieved by means of contortions and amazing acrobatic feats. It's not achieved by running longer, faster and harder. Rather, I believe balance is attained through some intentional reflection and careful choices. That's right, intentional reflection and careful choices. I decided to write it twice in order for us to slow down and really think about it.

Living a balanced life, a life of rhythm, requires that we be intimately connected to our passion and purpose. We have to understand what God has called us and designed us to do so that we can make these intentional choices that will lead to balanced living. Do you believe God has given you a unique calling, a sense of mission that is unique to you?  To answer this question, we must first go through some reflection time. We need to take regular times of silence and solitude, which are both forgotten arts in our culture, yet are critical skills for having a sense of balance and rhythm to your life.

## The Raft

Why do we need to commit to regular times of silence and solitude, times alone to struggle with the quiet?  So we can figure out how to stay in the raft. Let me explain. When I think about balance, I think of rafting in the Taylor River near Gunnison, Colorado. We were at a family reunion and, one afternoon, we decided to hit the river. Our oldest son, Drew, was all of three years old at the time. As a first-time dad, I was eager to expose him to as much "fun" as possible. Don't ask me to explain why, but we decided to take him on the river that day. The rafting started fast and hard; many boulders, turns and drops were immediately in our face. Drew was terrified and began to cry hysterically within two minutes from the start of the trip.

Our guide had boasted of guiding white water raft trips all over the world and was confident in telling us not to worry even though we had a young one on board. The guide said that he had never fallen out of a raft. Well, within five minutes, while my wife and I were more worried about a screaming child than the large boulder that lay in our path, we ignored the guide's instruction and failed to lean into the rock. We hit the rock dead on, spun and, consequently, launched the rafting guide out of the back of the boat like a slingshot into the rushing rapids. He was harassed relentlessly by his fellow rafting guides for the rest of the day. However, it was actually our failure to lean into the obstacle in front of us and our failure to balance the raft during that intense moment that caused our raft to go off course and cost our very seasoned guide his reputation. What was so critical for success on that rafting trip was the ability to balance the weight in the raft, listen, learn, anticipate and, above all, lean into the obstacles that were waiting for us in the river; not try and avoid them. The same principles apply to our lives.

It is easy for me to think of that raft when I contemplate the balance that exists in my own life. We had a three year old in the raft and hit a boulder broadside. Though our guide ended up swallowing some water and bruising his ego, I can think of far worse things that could have happened that day.

When I think of my "personal" raft, I know how important it is to keep the priorities in the right place. During the journey, things can shift and it will be critical for me to attend to one of the many areas of my life and make sure it's in the right place. Too little or too much attention could be costly and may result in a raft that capsizes because of a critical error. This is where reflection comes in. Stop for a moment and think about your raft. What has shifted and is in need of adjustment? Are there things in your raft that are clearly connected to your passion and purpose? Is each item spaced correctly in proportion to the others? If you aren't sure you know the answers to these questions, the first step toward a balanced life might be to close this book, spend a couple of hours sitting quietly alone with God and ask Him what He wants to tell you about your raft. Remember, in a raft there are people of all shapes, sizes and ages. Not everything can be the same. The important thing is to get people in the right place, depending on their interest, skill levels and size.

Each person in my imaginary raft represents a different aspect of my life that is a priority for an area of focus. Some of the weighty things in my raft include:

My relationship with my wife and kids

Hope for financial independence

Friends and key relationships

Fun and exercise

Having a high-impact work life

Investing deeply in a few key people

Your situation may sound a bit different, but the important thing is that you know what's in the raft. That sounds simple, but many people have difficulty clearly articulating the priorities in their life. The challenge for all of us is not only to name our priorities, but to live our life so that our actions reflect them as well. By observing your life, could those individuals close to you tell what your priorities are? Would their observations match what you might say about yourself? Why don't you ask a couple of people and see what they say?

## The Spiritual Side of the Raft

You may have noticed the raft in my illustration didn't mention my relationship with God. This is intentional. It seems to me that people who truly live with balance don't place God as simply another priority on their checklist or a separate object on the raft. He is in and around everything, He is what allows me to support or carry the other areas of my life. A balanced life, a life that has a sense of rhythm, is built around a relationship with God that can endure deep waters. Let me say I do not make that statement lightly. Right now my family is in the most difficult and turbulent waters of our lives. It is a time of deep questioning and soul searching. But, in these dark times, my heart tells me to keep the boat balanced, especially now when the waters are this rough.

In times like this, if my relationship becomes too shallow or inauthentic or if I place too much focus on what's in the raft instead of the raft and the water itself, the raft is in serious danger of capsizing. This relationship requires intentional investment and a fierce commitment to hang on. I really want to be known as someone who pursues Jesus.

Like any journey, there have been times in the wilderness: times when the pursuit has seemed boring and even irrelevant. Yes, there have been times when I have seriously questioned my faith and was close to walking away. Times when doubts, questions and struggles with God's apparent silence were nearly too much to keep going. There were also times when I had an amazing amount of energy and a desperate need to keep going.

Either way, through the years, I have used different methods to spur me on in this pursuit. At times, I read the Bible. At other times, I read books that challenge me and stretch my thinking. I'll take a long bike ride, get into His creation, have a good laugh and make sure I have times of quiet, just to listen. If I do one thing in my pursuit of God for too long, it tends to get ritualistic and my passion begins to wane. To battle this and not let myself slip into mediocrity, I do my best to mix it up. I encourage you to be creative and free in your thinking. Find things that will help draw you close to God. Don't put your spiritual life in a box, don't try and limit the amazing ways He could reveal Himself to you. I've experienced insight and had profound moments in a lot of surprising ways: through nature, movies, books and music from a wide variety of artists. In fact, one of the great "worship" moments of my life was at a U2 concert, shortly after the 9/11 tragedy. Bono may or may not have known it, but he led my friends and me in some real worship that night. Just don't get stuck; be open to new experiences, be honest with your pathway to God and do what it takes to get there.

My dad's heart seemed to be aligned with God as he took that quiet walk around the farm following the hailstorm that devastated his crops. It was not his first walk like this by any means. He had been through countless walks and conversations with God prior to that event. His day-to-day conversational relationship with God made all the difference as he went through life. He lived life with a quiet peace and a real, personal day-to-day walk that made him different, steady and balanced. He also kept his eyes and ears open, on alert for what may come his way.

Always be listening and watching, ready for God to speak to you no matter what you're doing. Some of my most profound "moments" have come when I least expected them! When you are relentless in your pursuit of this relationship, you're able to recognize His voice more easily.

When I was in third grade, I was watching the movie, "To Sir, with Love,"[1] a 1967 film starring Sidney Poitier as a reluctant teacher. In one scene, he stands in front of a classroom full of students who want to be there even less than he does. He drops his books into a trash can and says something like, "Today we put the books aside, and we start learning about real life." It was as if God spoke straight into my young heart and said, "Get ready. We're going beyond the books and outside the box." That was one of my favorite themes from childhood. I knew God had started me on a journey, drawing me to be part of an amazing process to influence life-change in other people. We will revisit this topic a bit later in the book. However, for now, let's take a few minutes to remember a time when you were really engaged in your walk with God. Where were you? Who were you with? What was going on in your life at that time? What disciplines or experiences were present that made your faith real, fresh and needed? Write down some of your thoughts.

Remember that insight can come through journaling, movies, friends or something that may totally surprise you. I often find that God communicates truth, love and beauty to me through nature. God may use many different things to communicate truth to you. I love to journal and, as a result, I spend quite a bit of time writing down my thoughts. I often put my pen to paper to record what I've been learning. It also helps me work through my doubts, struggles and questions. It is critical to find a time and a place to process through all that life offers us.

The most valuable thing I've done to keep my relationship with God vibrant has been scheduling personal retreats into my life on a regular basis. Every couple of months, I try to take a whole day to listen to God, all by myself. During these times, I may pray, quiet myself, journal, read, sleep, bike, hike or simply listen to music. Often I'll just wait. In the quiet, still moments there is space for God to speak. Over the years, when I've taken the time to give God my undivided attention, He has often given me the direction and insight I needed. I plan for these times, prepare for them, fight for them and fully expect Him to meet me and speak to my soul.

Another source of direction on my spiritual journey comes from a few close friends. To the best of their ability, these friends are committed to my spiritual journey. They ask me the hard questions. They are the ones who challenge me in multiple areas of my life and call me out when they sense I'm coasting. These are guys that I just enjoy having as friends on the journey of life as well. In times past, when I missed the balance of these relationships, I was often headed for trouble.

### What's in Your Raft?

With the raft in place, how do you determine what should be worth carrying? Each item in the raft should represent a clear priority in your life – something you are willing to pour yourself into, something that is worth your time, effort and emotional investment. Don't overcrowd your raft or things will begin to fall out. Keep it simple. Identify four or five priorities and re-evaluate these priorities often. At different seasons of life, you will have different people or items in your raft; you will have different passions and focuses so make sure you adjust accordingly.

Here is a glimpse of the contents of my raft. First is the relationship I have with my family. For me, family has been a priority since day one. I've made a commitment to God and to myself that no matter how fruitful the work or how great the opportunity, regardless of the distractions (good or bad), I am going to put these relationships first. Certainly, there have been times I have messed this up, but as a husband and a dad, I have an incredible opportunity to impact my family. This impact far outweighs any other relational impact I will ever have.

I am aware of the small window of opportunity I have to be with our kids and I don't want to miss it! I long to take all the time I can to be on the journey with them, to create memories and build relationships that will last a lifetime.

I put that priority into practice early in our children's lives. I was taking our oldest son, Drew, on bike rides and to ball games when he was two years old. He went on his first long hike in Colorado when he was just a year old, thanks to a backpack that I haven't been able to part with to this day. And I've already told you about the raft ride ... not recommended for a young one. When our children were small, I frequently took them with me to events that were part of my work with Youth for Christ/Campus Life. I realized that quality times were not going to happen without quantity. We had a blast going to lots of different events together. It was fun to include them in my work any chance I had. I love being a father. I try to soak up every moment and grab hold of every possible opportunity.

I was privileged to have a great role model in this area. Throughout my life, my mom, sisters and I never doubted that family was an absolute priority to my dad. He was always there for us. Even in his busy times at work, he was available. I always knew that he would stop what he was doing if I needed him, whether he was in the middle of harvest or in the middle of a football game.

Without a doubt, family was a priority to him, but he didn't limit his focus there. He still had time to run a successful farm and invest deeply in friendships with several other men, a rarity for his generation and occupation. Part of the secret in keeping his life in balance was that he knew the importance of focusing on different parts of his raft at certain times. Solomon really addressed this principle in Ecclesiastes 3:1-2, 4. It's one of the great pictures in the Bible on how to live life with a sense of rhythm. He wrote, "There is a time for everything, a season for every activity under heaven ... a time to plant and a time to uproot ... a time to weep and a time to laugh, a time to mourn and a time to dance." And, as I learned from my dad, there is also a time to fish.

The plains of Nebraska, the location of my father's farm, can be arid and dry. The crops almost always require irrigation, a very time-consuming task. My dad told me that whenever there was an inch or more of rain he could slow down the irrigation wells and take time to go fishing. Over the years, I made many laps out to the rain gauge to see if an inch had fallen. Do you see what he taught me here? Without saying a word, he taught me that there is a time to work and a time to play; a time to be focused on goals and a time to enjoy moments with your family. By his actions, he demonstrated that I wasn't the only thing, but I was important. Even today, because of his single illustration of what it means to live a life that's balanced, I still feel a sense of excitement and my heart still races when a thunderstorm passes. Over the last few years, I've enjoyed spending a lot of time fishing with our boys near the same dam where my dad and I used to catch white bass. However, I have other things on my raft that can't be ignored.

One item I'm paying close attention to is the area of financial independence. This is an ongoing challenge that continually changes. It's not about being rich or having a lot of stuff. For me, it's not even about the topic of money itself. In my raft, financial independence is about freeing me up to have more of a choice in what I do and how I invest my time.

Too often we lose the rhythm to our lives because we make financial decisions that trap us with debt. We buy a house that's bigger than what we need or a car that's a bit more fancy than we can afford. I can tell you with certainty that, over the years, I have wasted too much money on cars and watched their value, and my investment, simply fade away. Spontaneous spending and credit card debt can quickly tip our entire raft and damage everything in it.

The place I would like to get to (I'm not there yet) is to be free from debt with investments that will return dollars to me down the road. I'd like to invest in such a way that I can have passive income that will free me from being enslaved to a particular job with a particular salary just so I can keep up with the bills.

God willing, someday, financial independence will allow me to invest my time in more strategic places. Getting there takes sacrifice, commitment and a willingness to take risks and live differently than those around us.

As I carefully and strategically attend to this part of my raft, I'm learning financial principles that will help me live a more balanced life. I summarized some of my new financial acumen for our then 18-year-old son, Drew, in a journal I wrote for him during his senior year in high school.

*Journal Entry, April 17, 2006*

**Make a commitment to do things differently than most of your friends.** *Specifically, tell yourself that you won't surrender to the "I want this and I want it now" mentality. Most of my spontaneous financial purchases have turned out to be bad decisions. I still learn this myself every day. Sometimes I succeed, sometimes I fail.*

**Make a commitment to be debt free on everything that does not increase in value.** *If you use a credit card, pay it off in full every month.*

**Invest in the future.** *I do my best to save ahead for cars and other purchases by putting just $50 to $100 dollars a month in a mutual* *fund. It's amazing how savings build up. Several years ago we bought a duplex to serve as a rental property. Even though many times it's been a real pain, it has been one of the best financial decisions I have made.*

***Place yourself around people who are successful in a financial, personal and business sense.** Learn from them and act on their advice. Remember, you tend to act like those you have in your company.*

***Start early and have staying power.** Keep investing and keep saving, not so you'll have money, but so you'll have more freedom in other life choices.*

I do my best to live by these principles today.

For me, living a life with rhythm is not a passive life. It is a life of purpose and impact. Impacting people is an important section of my raft. I need to know that my life is making a difference; that I am accomplishing what God has designed me to do.

I want to take advantage of every opportunity I am given to positively impact people. During much of my life, ministry has been my job, but impact goes far beyond what I do vocationally. I want to be a faithful boss, friend, youth sports coach and dad. As God lays various opportunities in front of me, I want to be ready to act on them.

One of the keys to having great impact is having great focus. I saw this truth often in my job at Campus Life. One of my most important roles there was to keep people focused on the core mission of Campus Life/Youth for Christ, which was to go into the world of teenagers and help them understand what it means to have a relationship with God. There were tons of good things that our staff could have done in working with teenagers, but if we wanted to have maximum impact, we needed to have a laser-like focus on the core mission of whatever we were doing. We had to say "no" to some good things that were outside of our focus or beyond our mission. If we spread ourselves too thin, we lose our impact. Things break easily when they are stretched too thin.

The final thing in my raft is the friends that walk through life with me. I'm a relational guy so this is very important to me, though it is not always easy. I naturally gravitate toward this and have had to learn when to turn off the spigot and focus on other things.

One thing that has been key to this area is identifying the different types of friendships. We need friends for the journey and friends at various stops along the way. Friends for the journey are those life-long friends in whom we deeply invest and who deeply invest in us. They are few and far between. When you have a friend who is deeply committed to your life journey and invests in you, do what it takes to stay engaged. There are friends along the way who will simply walk with us for a portion of the journey. Trying to determine which friends to invest in has sometimes been a difficult lesson for me. In the past, I sometimes made the mistake of keeping too many things going and stringing people along in order to fit everybody in and avoid anyone feeling "left out." Even though my heart has always been in the right place, it has caused hurt feelings and conflict over the years. I'm learning to be more intentional, avoiding doing too much and trying not to please everyone. You can't please everyone all the time and that goes for friendships as well. Trying to include everybody has often hurt me more than others in the long run.

I've also learned the hard way that conflict with friends can tip the raft. If I don't quickly resolve conflicts and deal with disappointments, I'm soon pouring way too much emotional energy into one part of the raft. I'm learning to do what it takes to get some resolution, let it go and then move on. Every human being is imperfect and flawed. To expect a relationship with another human being to be free of discord would be an inaccurate and disappointing reality. The only way to avoid these disappointments is to avoid relationships. I don't think that is an option we can afford to take; none of us were created to live life alone. Yes, there have been deep disappointments in friendships over the years, but I have learned to embrace those times and enter into relationships to grow, share life, forgive and bring the other person to a higher place.

Once again, my dad was my role model when it comes to friendships. He had many deep friendships, particularly for a man of his generation. He was unusual in that regard. Most guys have limited friendships. They either don't know how to develop friendships or are unwilling to make it a priority. However, at my dad's funeral, four or five different men came up to me and told me that they had lost their best friend that day.

When my dad passed away, he left me a map in the way he lived his life. He always seemed to be in rhythm. He left behind a wife, a son and two daughters who knew they were loved and valued. He left an impression on his nieces and nephews who loved him like their own father; they were deeply impacted by him and speak fondly of him to this day. He left friends who still speak of the impact he had on their lives. He left a successful business that has continued to provide financially for his family. He didn't rush through life, rely on easy solutions or avoid difficult questions. The way he lived his life just seemed to have rhythm. He listened and prepared for the rough waters. He was often still and quiet; he didn't juggle, walk a tight rope or struggle to keep his raft afloat. He wasn't in constant stress or worry about falling or tipping his raft. What he did do, though, was take time for some long, slow walks with God.

STOP TWO   -   KNOW THE HORIZON

# KNOW THE HORIZON

*Navigation is the fine art of looking ahead while successfully rowing through the water you're in right now.*

I wasn't ready. This fatherhood thing was bearing down on me fast and I was a little nervous. Okay, I was very nervous. I turned to the man I trusted most to understand my fears—my dad. When I told him that Marcia and I were expecting a baby, he looked at me and said, "It's going to be a boy and you're going to have a blast." I had no idea those would be some of the last words I'd hear my father speak. Our oldest child, Drew, was born the day after what would have been my father's 60th birthday.

There I was, in my mid-20s, embarking on a new part of the journey and I had suddenly lost my compass, my bearing, my beacon. I felt unprepared, lonely and on my own.

*Journal Entry, June 17, 1987*

*In a few days I will become a dad. Our first baby is due on what would have been by dad's 60th birthday. I walk through the hospital and see all of the excited grandparents, and I realize that this is the first big event of my life that my dad will miss, and that stinks.*

*What a mix of excitement, anticipation and sadness at the same time.*

*The stab of grief brings a ton of questions and some regret. "God, help me not to take for granted, even in the slightest way, the people and experiences you have given me. I really miss my dad and I wish I had done some things differently. But help me embrace the opportunities ahead as best as I can."*

*My dad was always there for the big moments. I remember a difficult high school basketball game. I had put so much into preparing for the game and looked forward to it for almost a year, and I didn't get to play much. When it was over, I was a jumbled mix of anger, embarrassment and disappointment. Instead of telling me what I could have done better or to work harder, he just listened and was "in" the moment with me. It seemed like he felt it as much as I did.*

*How can I replace that?*

*I have to believe that God is with me and cares even more than my dad did, but that is hard to do. I will never forget the deep impact he had on me. I hope I can pass that impact on to my soon-to-be-born child. I feel compelled to somehow keep it going.*

*I have a ton of questions, and it is hard to see God in this, but I do look ahead to a homecoming in heaven when we can catch some extended time. That will be a day when this hurt and emptiness fades away; it will be a good celebration for sure. Until then, God help me give it my best shot. Help me to have at least some of the impact on my friends, my family and the teenagers I work with as my dad had on me, and so many others.*

Yes, the journey has a way of taking us to many places we don't feel prepared to go. And we need to ready ourselves for whatever life has in store for us and not let ourselves get stuck.

The truth is, we need to keep moving even though we won't always know what lies ahead. It's like the words to one of my favorite Tom

Petty songs "It's time to move on, time to get going; what lies ahead I have no way of knowing."[1] In fact, many times we have no idea where we are going and we will feel unprepared and often very alone. Nevertheless, one thing's for sure: we will never find the way if we are stuck, stagnant and void of any growth. On my life journey I think of many times that I have deviated from the predictable straight path. This is often where the real adventure begins. Journeys involve movement. Journeys involve change. Risk is part of the equation—and so are excitement, adventure, disappointment, surprise, loss, spontaneity, grief and anticipation. For those of us who focus on the destination, who long for the security of a well-marked map and the stability of a predictable estimated time of arrival, this is unsettling news. However, this is the reality we all face. We can try to protest, pull back and choose not to participate in the journey, but even when we stop going forward, life just moves on. Just ask Mitch Robins, the middle-aged guy played by Billy Crystal in the 1991 movie, "City Slickers":

> *"Value this time in your life kids, because this is the time in your life when you still have your choices, and it goes by so quickly. When you're a teenager you think you can do anything, and you do. Your 20s are a blur. Your 30s, you raise your family, you make a little money and you think to yourself, 'What happened to my 20s?' Your 40s, you grow a little potbelly, you grow another chin. The music starts to get too loud and one of your old girlfriends from high school becomes a grandmother. Your 50s you have a minor surgery. You'll call it a procedure, but it's a surgery. Your 60s you have a major surgery, the music is still loud but it doesn't matter because you can't hear it anyway. Seventies, you and the wife retire to Fort Lauderdale; you start eating dinner at two, lunch around 10, breakfast the night before. And you spend most of your time wandering around malls looking for the ultimate in soft yogurt and muttering, 'How come the kids don't call?' By your 80s, you've had a major stroke, and you end up babbling to some Jamaican nurse who your wife can't stand but who you call mama. Any questions?"[2]*

Like Mitch, we're all on a road traveling from life stage to life stage. We can choose to sit at the side of the road and watch our lives pass by, like cars on a lonesome highway, complaining and wondering where the time has gone, or we can engage and embrace the journey—even when it surprises us, confuses us and disappoints us.

One of the struggles of my life that comes to mind is my mom's cancer. She died of lung cancer at age 62, just a few years after my dad's death. My mom was a bit of a mystic. She actually believed that God spoke to her through dreams and revelations. She prayed passionately for people and actually had the audacity to believe God answered those prayers, even to the extent of seeing people healed. For example, as a child, my niece had been diagnosed by multiple physicians in Hastings and Omaha, with what looked to be a fatal kidney disease. To the amazement of doctors, she was completely healed. No doubt in my mind that, in part, God honored the relentless prayers and the passionate pursuits of my mother. As she was driving to our hometown one day, she felt a strong impression to go see a woman she had been meeting with in another city. In my mom's words, the woman had the look of death to her and was, in fact, moments away from ending her own life. What would have happened if my mom had not responded to the prompting of God? She just always seemed dialed in.

Yet my mom, at a relatively young age, faced the battle of her life. I remember not going to a prayer service others were having for her because I just couldn't face the disappointment if she wasn't able to overcome this disease. The hurt and disappointment in God did come and it was painful to watch the cancer systematically take her out.

In fact, the journey does take us to many places, places of depth and excitement and yes, some very dark places as well. Are you ready? Are you ready for the unpredictable twists and turns that will certainly come? Are you ready to face the impact of various seasons of life? I look at things very differently at age 45 than I did at age 25. It would have been great to have someone walk with me through the mountains and valleys. It would have been even better to have had a guide to help me anticipate those mountains and valleys, to teach me and show me how to prepare and respond – a person who had staying power and wisdom to help me avoid being crushed by the relentless obstacles in front of me.

As I write this chapter, our daughter, Ali, just started college. I'm excited to see her fully engage in the adventure that lies before her. In the past few months, I've had a front-row seat as she makes decisions that will determine part of her journey. Like all of us she has made her fair share of both poor and great choices. Some of those choices and their consequences gave us great opportunity to engage many life issues with her. And, as it goes with many teens, some of those great choices can often lead to some painfully lonely Friday and Saturday nights. But she kept moving, kept learning and growing through those messy and sometimes tough years of high school. I will always be thankful for Caitlin and the other Campus Life staff members who came alongside Ali to listen and help guide her. Caitlin had been in the same situation and walked the road a few years before. She helped Ali anticipate what was ahead and always reminded her that she was bigger than the pressures and issues that were pressing in on her.

When our son graduated a few years ago from high school, I wrote this in a journal I made for him:

*Journal Entry, April 18, 2005*

*Today you're deciding on whether or not to go to Colorado to try out for a Division II basketball team in Denver. It will be interesting to see what you do. I hope you will give it a shot to see what happens because you've always wanted to play college basketball. Either way, I support you. I do want you to live life with a sense of adventure and readiness to take risks and try new things. In my past there are things that I wished I had tried. Sometimes I wish I would have pushed out of my comfort zone sooner in work and my personal life to create new challenges and get things stirred up.*

*You are not afraid of risk and trying new things, but you will have to challenge yourself not to coast, not to get too comfortable, to push into new areas, challenging yourself mentally, socially, physically and spiritually to do things with excellence.*

*Live life with no regrets. I saw a survey once of people in their 80s who said consistently the two things they would change about their lives are that they would spend more time with their families and they would take more risks and try new things.*

*Use the next years to seek out how God wants to use you. Try new things. Get a variety of experiences. Don't settle for the easiest route.*

*See where the road takes you. Don't settle just for what's comfortable or familiar. Don't always look for the straight path through the wilderness. These are the words of challenge and encouragement I want our kids to remember. They are the same words I want to remember. They are the same words my Father is whispering to me, especially when the journey takes me places I don't feel prepared to go.*

## Faith and Fear During the Journey

A couple of years ago I saw a video where Curt Lehman, the founding pastor of a now large church, addressed his congregation at a point of transition with these words: "Growth produces change, which can lead to insecurity. Insecurity leads to fear. And unchecked, fear can lead to inactivity and immobility."

The fear part of that equation is very real for all of us and has been very real for me as our children reach key transition points in their journeys. When our son, Drew, was 15, he wanted to pursue his dream of playing basketball at one of the biggest high schools in our state.

We had recently moved to an acreage outside of town so our children could attend a smaller, perhaps safer (in our minds) school system, a school in which we felt he would have more opportunities to play and participate. However, Drew longed for a huge challenge and a bigger stage.

My wife and I prayed about the decision and wrestled with the implications. It was hard to give up our well-ordered plans. We dealt with insecurity and fear: fear of a different peer group, fear that he might not make the team, let alone get a starting position. What if this? What if that? There were so many things to think about! After much thought, we decided that we needed to look at the way God had made Drew. We needed to take into account his unique abilities, personality, dreams and strengths. We didn't just risk blindly. We let Drew try out for a select team with many of the players who attended the school he had his heart set on. We watched how he played with them. We talked to the coaches about his abilities and his chance to succeed. We asked God for wisdom in parenting Drew, then took a deep breath and made the best decision we could. We let him choose his own high school. Even though at the time it was out of our comfort zone and a big risk, time has shown us the bigger risk would have been not to let him make the change.

I had a good friend once tell me if you have children who are risk takers, it's good to let them take some risks while they are still at home. There is a lot of wisdom in that method and we tried to apply it with our risk-taking kids. A parent's tendency is to protect, coddle and keep them safe at all costs, but it's really important to let them push out, take risks and absorb the consequences of those risks while they are at home and you are able to walk through everything with them. If you control things too tightly, there may be some tough times ahead when they do move out. As parents, we have to wrestle with this and find a balance between being protective and allowing our kids to take risks and we must get a grip on our own fear and faith.

These constant tug-of-wars between faith and fear are part of the journey. I now believe they may be the very essence of the journey. They are what move us from the smooth, flat plains to the heights and depths of our lives. Fear and risk will always be part of the journey. We must decide if they will be detours or dead ends that simply take us out.

My father taught my older sister, Michele, how to win the tug of war between faith and fear. Like so many valuable lessons, it was taught "along the way" as we lived life in our Nebraska farmhouse. Michele tells the story:

> *"When I was little, I was deathly afraid of thunderstorms. Deathly is not an exaggeration. At the first sound of thunder I would run down the stairs and get in bed with mom and dad. As the storm would increase, Dad would want to get up to survey everything. Dad was my protector. So I would get up with him. I would walk behind him, my arms wrapped around his waist, walking step for step with him. Although I was scared to death, I felt safe at the same time. I knew that Dad would not lead me into any sort of danger. When the lightning would flash and the thunder would crash, I would just hold tighter. We would walk from window to window, him watching, me clinging.*

> *"Now, 'my protector' is gone. But what he taught me through that is invaluable. I am always bent toward fear. I deal with it all of the time, but I have learned to run to my Father. I cling to Him. When the lightning of life strikes and thunder of fear rumbles through, I hold tighter. I walk step for step with my Father watching the storm around me, sometimes nearly crippled by fear, but all the while knowing that He will not lead me anywhere where He cannot protect me. He is my safety. Dad could have thought it was a very silly thing having this child clutching to him as he was surveying the storm. He could have*

*told me to go back to my own bed, that nothing was going to happen, He could have done a lot of things, but what he did taught me one of the most valuable lessons of my life."*[3]

We are not alone on this journey even when all we can see is the storm. I was skiing a few years ago in Steamboat Springs, Colorado, with our kids. It had snowed off and on throughout the morning. After lunch we headed to the upper slopes. By the time we got on the first run, it was a total whiteout. We could only see a few feet in front of us. It's hard to keep moving in the midst of the storm, hard to trust the map, guidance of other people or even your own abilities when you can't see what lies ahead or around you.

I wonder if that's actually the good that comes from walking through the storms in life that come our way. When I can't see my way out, I am forced to trust something beyond myself, something deeper and more significant. No matter what the outcome, I have to believe that God will walk with me every step of the way.

Through all the changes and transitions of life, those same storms help me to remember that God is timeless and His character never changes. He has promised to never leave us or forsake us no matter what. Life may not turn out like we want, but He's not going to ditch us along the way. He's said He'll be a constant companion on the journey. He also gives us other companions along the way.

## Enlisting the Help of Guides Along the Way

Imagine going on a trip to Arizona. You're driving along Highway 64 between Tucson and Desert View. You keep your eyes on the road. You've never been there before and the road is unfamiliar. You don't look to your left and you miss it. You miss the Grand Canyon. You didn't even know it was there. You sped right past the best part of the trip because you hadn't asked anyone who'd been down that road what you should see along the way. Take time to learn what's ahead on the journey. Take initiative. Meet someone who's a few steps ahead of you for a beer or coffee. Be intentional, get ahead of the game and don't forget to share what you've learned along the way with those who are a few steps behind you.

Too many of us forget this. We become so self-absorbed that we forget the deep impact others have had on us at various parts of the journey. More importantly, we don't take the time to give back to others, to come alongside others who may be a few steps behind us. Take some time now to pause and think . . . do you remember the key people who impacted your life? Who were they? What was going on in your life when they emerged? How would you describe or characterize their impact? Journal what comes to mind. Don't rush this. Take some time to linger here. Put the book down. Write down the names, the places and the qualities that come to mind.

This exercise is critical for many reasons. First of all, it will encourage you; it will serve as a reminder that God has not forgotten you. Hopefully, it will inspire you to keep going and continue to pour into others as well. We'll look more at that a bit later.

When our family went on a trip to New York, we were fortunate enough to have a family member as a guide who knew the side roads and places to go. We were staying in Upper Manhattan and our goal for the day was to see the Statue of Liberty in Lower Manhattan. Rather than rush right to the statue, we took a course that led in that general direction but was full of experiences along the way. If we had focused solely on reaching our destination, we would have missed the most exciting day of the entire trip. We would have missed a great brunch in a corner cafe in Greenwich Village. I would have missed an amazing conversation with someone who had been in the area during the 9/11 tragedy. We would have missed the memorial service honoring the rescue workers held each afternoon at a little Methodist church that was once nestled in the shadow of the Twin Towers. We would have missed a great view down Wall Street, shopping in Chinatown, and some fantastic pizza in Little Italy. Maybe if we slow down enough, we will find that the journey is where we find the purpose, the passion, the energy and the spark to keep us moving.

God tells us He'll take care of the path. Proverbs 3:6 says, "In all your ways acknowledge Him and He will make your paths straight." He will pave the way. Our job is to stay focused, keep moving and learn from people who have already traveled the road. There is no teacher like experience and we can learn from the experience of others as well as our own. Listen to others, absorb whatever you can. Anticipate and plan for changes and the seasons of life that lie in front of you. Your ability to do this is critical and will help you avoid some of the pitfalls and traps of the enemy that await you in the years to come.

That's part of why I miss my dad so much. I wish I could have asked him about the struggles, the traps and the questions of mid-life. It might have saved me some heartache. I want to know why he let me get in a car with a friend and move to Colorado with no money and no job when I was just 18. Was he crazy? I want to know how he grew older without growing jaded. I want to know if he had any regrets. I want him to show me how to navigate this season of life.

Over the years, God has placed people in my path who have walked ahead of me, then slowed down long enough to tell me what they've learned. One of those men is my dad's friend, George Osborne. He has always helped me remember. He keeps me grounded and centered. He is one of the men I talk to when I need to make a big decision.

I have also had others who have spoken into many areas of my life. There were the veterans of Youth for Christ who I would connect with. When the challenges of leading a large organization and the pressure of fundraising was so heavy, they seemed to always have a story and words of encouragement. They would remind me to stay on track and to be relentlessly committed to the mission. They would remind me that it was mavericks that founded YFC and challenged me to not lose that part of me; even as the organization continued to grow. They were people who pursued God hard and thought and dreamed outside the box themselves. I needed to be around people like that. I always left my time with them more centered, ready to not just hang on, but to step into whatever God had for me next.

Then there was the man I often talked to about transitions, and how you know when it's time for a change, time to move on to the next challenge. Once, he told me that you know it is time to move on when your vision and new ideas start to dry up, when you start to feel like a stranger in your own organization, when others offer more vision than you. This looks different for everyone, but I knew I did not want to wait too long; which is a mistake many leaders make. A few years later, I realized how sage that advice was when I changed course after leading an organization for 15 years.

It's been my experience that mentors (at least the ones really worth listening to) don't show up on the doorstep saying, "Let me impart my vast wisdom and knowledge to you." We must pursue these "come alongside people." Look for people who are navigating their careers, their family life and their relationships in ways that you admire. Look for people who have traveled a road you now find yourself on. Ask them to be a compass for you. Like I said earlier, be ready to share your stories and lessons of the road with others as well. We all need others to come alongside us at critical times and in the pivotal moments.

One thing I've learned from those ahead of me is that the journey requires constant adjustments. What keeps us afloat during one life stage may drown us in another. We must learn to adjust our sails as the wind blows in new directions.

What would happen if a 40-year-old father with three young children tried to navigate his journey like a 20-year-old college student? Several years ago my son and I were exploring colleges and were on a campus tour of Colorado State University. Halfway into the tour I was stoked. The campus was great, the mountains were beautiful and I soon realized that I was experiencing the campus in "first person." I quickly reminded myself, "This is about Drew; this isn't for you. In fact, you will be paying a very expensive tuition bill if he goes here." My 20-something excitement soon turned to a 40-something reality!

If we fail to plan, anticipate and adjust to the impact of the different seasons of life, we could be in real trouble. If I don't plan now to keep my long-term relationship with God, my wife and my vision for life, fresh, passionate and moving, then there certainly will be hard times ahead.

Personally, I had a lot more time to devote to friends, work and even ministry at age 25. I could sail with a little lighter hand on the wheel and ride the rapids with more reckless abandon. Once I became a husband and a father, I had to make some adjustments in my raft. I had to draw my boundaries in a little tighter to protect family time and plan my course a little more methodically to avoid the kind of sudden shifts in direction that might send my wife or family overboard. Failure to make adjustments in my time, schedule and priorities would have been devastating to my family. We all know of others who have failed to adjust along the way and, often, it's their families that pay a serious price.

## Age and the Journey

A few years ago, I failed to prepare for the impact of being a 40-something. I entered a period of restless boredom. I was bored in relationships, bored at work, and tried in my faith. I struggled to find excitement and adventure somewhere in life. This kind of restless boredom can lead in a couple of different directions. It can lead to a train wreck. We all know people who have gone this direction. It can also lead to a time of creating and discovering something new, something deeper in our relationship with God, family and work. Sometimes it is both. For me, this was perhaps the most difficult time of my life. Though I was unprepared and undeserving, God showed me His grace, woke me up before I really messed things up, didn't let me stay in the dark place that I found myself and showed me that real life can only come from a deep, more intentional pursuit of Jesus.

As a result, a new adventure was developed, one that ties together the themes of my life – Harbor Ministries. This ministry is designed to help young leaders, and those in mid-life, live a life of rhythm, leave a legacy and finish well. It's a dream and a vision, born out of my own leadership journey, shaped out of my own mistakes and successes. It's a dream that God put on my heart at my lowest point, in my darkest days in the wilderness. Believe me, this is a stage of life and leadership that you desperately need to prepare for!

We need to understand the impact both our age and life-stage have on our journey. We've got to monitor our emotional, physical and spiritual gauges and adjust our direction and pace accordingly. A wise man or woman will look ahead and anticipate coming life-stages and plan how to navigate through them. Navigation is the fine art of looking ahead while successfully rowing through the water you're in right now. The only way I know how to accomplish this is to take time out on a regular basis to get a reading on where I'm at and how I'm doing. I continue to look ahead to others who have been through the waters I'm trying to navigate right now.

It's important that we don't let our own planning, seeking wisdom from others, and even pursuing God become an attempt to assure that we'll always have smooth sailing along a well-defined course. We have to remember that, no matter how prepared, planned or structured we are, there will still be times of surprising joy and excitement as well as deep sorrow and loneliness. This is the essence of the journey. In fact, I'm not talking about a step-by-step plan or an inflexible structure. Life has a way of trashing even our best plans. I'm talking about an awareness — a depth and a strength that will allow you to be resilient and steady through the many seasons of life.

Several years ago, I was trying to figure out what to do with my next set of years. Nearing 40, I needed to know that God cared about my future and would show me the straight way I had lost. In my journal I wrote:

> *I need to have a willingness to go through the wilderness and for a long time I've not been able to see my way out. But faith says soon enough God will allow me to emerge from the wilderness and I will come out on a plateau, and a valley with a single track-like path will emerge in front of me. Direction is clear. No need to wrestle with choices. It will be God's reward for enduring the wilderness.*

That single, track-like path I envisioned is continually emerging through the creation of Harbor Ministries. What also emerged was something I longed for and needed much more than a clear road map to my future. What I've found is that the mystery of God and His path for me, keeps me coming back to Him again and again.

*Journal Entry, February 4, 2004*

> *A fantastic walk under the stars last night! I could see and experience God in so many ways. God is so big yet so intimately involved with us. More than anything, I just need to walk with God, fight the spiritual warfare but then simply walk with God. Listen. Be ready to respond when He does speak. And know that the walk, the journey, the conversation with God is what He wants with me, as well as what I want. It's time to take the pressure off and go on this journey of life with Jesus.*

*An observation that resonated today was that the reason God doesn't lay out the plan for us is because we would just go about it. By unveiling one thing at a time, by retaining the great mystery of our lives, it causes us to seek God, to walk with Him throughout our lives. (Psalm 32:8, Psalm 25: 12-14, John 15:15)*

*But there is a plan and our job is to decipher this code to gain understanding into God's plan for our life as it continually unfolds. And remember, His calling is not a place, not a position. It is the rhythm of your life. To find that is a great adventure.*

I once heard a story of a father who took his son hiking. They had spent time planning the trip for many weeks. The son had carefully filled his small pack and waited on the front steps for his dad to arrive home from work so their journey could begin. The plan called for the father and son to hike a few miles up the mountain and make camp before sunset. But things ran late at work and traffic was heavy on the way out of town. During the drive the father rubbed his temple, cursed the traffic and turned up the baseball game on the radio. The son never took his eyes off his father. When they started their hike, the father was impatient. His son had to stop to use the bathroom, then to tie his shoe. At one point the son stopped to watch a snake poke its head in and out of its hole. The father grew impatient and urged his son to hurry. They had to make it to the campsite. The father walked faster. The son had to almost run to keep up. At times the father had to verbally push and drag him along so they could move even faster. When they did get to the camp, the father hurried to pitch the tent and warm a can of soup. Through the glow of the hastily made fire, he caught a glimpse of his weary son asleep on the ground, with tear stains on his cheeks. At that moment, he knew he had missed it. He may have reached the destination, but he had missed the journey.[4]

I don't want to miss the great moments along the way. I don't want to screw up my life by failing to anticipate the impact of various parts of the journey.

There is a stretch of road that is a beautiful desert drive in Utah. You can be so taken by the natural beauty around you that you could miss a very important sign that says, "No gas for over 100 miles." It is a wild, raw, gorgeous stretch of desert highway, but it is a stretch of road that I wouldn't want to walk! And while I want to take in all that is around me, I also don't want to get lost and lose part of my life because I failed to anticipate and prepare. At the same time, if we miss the journey, if we fail to pause, laugh, enjoy, evaluate and ready ourselves for what lies ahead, we could become stagnant or, even worse, we become headed for a painful crash. You have to keep moving or you will certainly miss the lessons of the road. Keep moving and engage the journey ahead of you. Otherwise you may lack the strength, inspiration, courage and depth needed to leave a legacy, to stay the course and finish well.

STOP THREE  -  DON'T DO THIS ALONE

# DON'T DO THIS ALONE

*Whatever you do, stay connected to the things, the people, the dreams that give you life.*

One of my favorite stories in the Bible is the story of Jonathan and the man that bore his armor, taking on the Philistine army in the fourteenth chapter of the first book of Samuel.

Jonathan said to his young armor-bearer, "Come, let us go over to the outpost of those uncircumcised fellows. Perhaps the Lord will act in our behalf. Nothing can hinder the LORD from saving, whether by many or by few." "Do all that you have in mind," his armor-bearer said. "Go ahead; I am with you heart and soul." (1 Samuel 14: 6–7)

It's an incredible story of courage, strength, companionship and faith. Jonathan is probably restless, frustrated and tired of doing nothing, so God prompts him to take action. He tells his armor-bearer something to the effect of, "We are going to engage the Philistine army. We are going to make something happen, the two of us against hundreds! With God on our side, I love our odds." Equally amazing to Jonathan's willingness to engage the enemy is the reaction of his armor-bearer. "Go for it!" he says, "Follow your heart. I'm with you!"

Their willingness to confront an incredible enemy changes everything. What I find equally amazing is the overwhelming trust these two must have had and the incredible bond they shared. In this case, they did not scale the mountain alone.

Most of us—especially men—don't take the time to connect and really invest in relationships that will last. We tend to walk through our days in an independent fog, acting as if life doesn't depend on meaningful connections with other people. If we want to truly grasp life as God originally intended, we have to believe, and know deep down in our gut, that we can't do this alone.

## Superhero Connections

When I was growing up, I loved the Lone Ranger, Zorro and Spiderman. In my mind, these independent mavericks could do it all. They could leap tall buildings, fend off evil, rescue the ladies in distress and hold back the forces of nature with their eyes closed, all while operating as a one-man show. They were the picture of masculinity for me at an early age. They were the men I wanted to be like. I often envisioned myself as a mountain man or an explorer, independent, strong, self-made, braving the brutal wilderness, all on my own, exhibiting strength and self-sufficiency. It wasn't that I didn't like people. In fact, I was very relational, often in the company of many friends. However, deep down, I admired those that I perceived to be "self-made survivors." These were the people who really didn't need anybody else—the people who had the confidence and resiliency to make it on their own no matter what obstacles they faced.

Amidst my envy of these self-sufficient heroes, I was missing part of the whole picture. Somehow, my young mind overlooked the fact that the Lone Ranger had a valuable partner (Tonto) and even Silver got the masked man out of more than one scrape. I love the way one of my favorite authors, John Eldredge, describes just how well-connected many heroes are in "Waking the Dead."

*"When Neo is set free from the Matrix, he joins the crew of the Nebuchadnezzar—the little hovercraft that is the headquarters and ship of the small fellowship called to set the captives free. There are nine of them in all, each a character in his own way, but nonetheless a company of the heart, a 'band of brothers,' a family bound together in a single fate. Together, they train for battle. Together, they plan their path. When they go back into the Matrix to set others free, each one has a role, a gifting, a glory. They function as a team. And they watch each other's back.*

*"You see this sort of thing at the center of every great story. Dorothy takes her journey with the Scarecrow, the Tin Woodman, the Lion, and of course, Toto. Maximus rallies his little band and triumphs over the greatest empire on earth. When Captain John Miller is sent deep behind enemy lines to save Private Ryan, he goes in with a squad of eight rangers. And, of course, Jesus had the twelve. This is written so deeply on our hearts: You must not go alone. The Scriptures are full of such warnings, but until we see our desperate situation, we hear it as an optional religious assembly for an hour on Sunday mornings."[1]*

No question, you were not meant to do this alone. Relationships are not optional for anyone who wants to truly thrive on this incredible and complex journey. Relationships provide critical checkpoints on the map of your life. Let those thoughts sink in for just a minute. Do you believe it? It is easy to say yes, but do you really believe that not letting others into your world and your story will rob them and you of the strength you need to run this race well?

## Deeply Connected

As a boy, I deeply admired my father. Though he is not here today, I still admire him—but my perception of him has changed. When I was young, he seemed to be the epitome of an independent, self-made man who rarely, if ever, needed the help of other people. Some of what I believed about him was true because on the last day of his life, when he needed the help of others the most, he still tried to do it alone. That refusal to get help and insistence that everything was all right may have cost him his life. However, what I didn't fully realize at the time was that he was actually a man of deep connections. He was closely connected to God, intimately involved in his family and had many close friends with whom he shared his life. These connections were the key source of his strength.

Remember that long, slow walk my dad took around the cornfield, shortly after the devastating hailstorm? Well, he didn't make that journey alone. His best friend, George Osborne, accompanied him for a portion of that walk. George and my dad had a deep influence on each other. Check out a letter he wrote to me a couple years ago, 20 years after my dad's death:

> *"My relationship with Lloyd could best be described as the ability in each of us to communicate with the other without talking. It was eerie. He gave me the most priceless gift one man can bestow on another: unconditional friendship. He let me see and share inside all the warts he thought he had, none of which I could see. He saw my inconsistencies as justifiable, he acted over my reluctances, he took me into places and relationships that I preferred not to go or do, he made me realize that often, if not always, a sense of humor and joy exceed wisdom and intellect. He was a real soul-mate."*

I still meet George for breakfast sometimes. It's been almost 25 years since my father passed away and their friendship still endures in the heart of George, as well as in the hearts of many others.

As I said earlier, my dad had many deep friendships which, for a man of his generation, was unusual. Actually, for a man of any generation, it is rare. At my dad's funeral, four or five different guys confessed to me that they had just lost their best friend. One of his pallbearers said, "I may have carried your dad today, but this is the only time. He basically carried me for 40 years. He kept me involved in church and engaged with my family. He can't be replaced."

Connections like that require effort. How did a man like George Osborne, who was busy with his career as a physician and raising a family, have time to forge an intimate, enduring relationship with my dad? I think he understood that, throughout life, all sorts of different connections are needed. It simply makes life fuller, deeper and more fun.

### Friends for the Journey

Friends for the journey are those few people who will walk through life with you. They will be there for you during different life-stages and seasons of your life. They will be there during the peaks and valleys, in deep disappointments, screw-ups and successes. So who has your back? Who do you have history with? Who is committed to being there for you and you for them in the future?

For over 10 years, there were four of us who had lunch almost every Tuesday. After my mom passed away, this group formed when I really sensed the need for support. What evolved was truly amazing. Over the past decade, we have had hundreds of lunches at our favorite spot, Yia Yia's Pizza. We've played golf, attended concerts, prayed together and laughed a lot!

Recently, these guys have plodded through some difficult life stages. Some of us have lost parents. Others have faced serious marriage, family and health issues. We have helped each one wrestle with tough spiritual questions and have walked through major vocational changes. We've done some things right. We've all done some things wrong. And, we've all made mistakes we regret. However, for the most part, we were there for each other, trying to help one another figure things out. A couple of years ago, a few of these guys joined me in celebrating my oldest son's final high school basketball game. He had his best game ever and they were there to share it with me.

Times change—we get together less frequently these days. Even though we are engaged in different battles and things are continually changing around us, we have generally had each other's back. In both the tough times and the great times, these are the guys I leaned on. We have history, we know each other's story, and we have bonded together by the extreme ups and downs of life.

I know that some of you reading this book haven't experienced this kind of friendship. I challenge you to seek out some people with whom you could have an intimate connection. It is not easy, I had to make the effort to initiate and build new relationships with people time and time again. It isn't random and it won't just happen. I invited these guys to lunch. I took risks. I made phone calls. Be intentional with people! Take a look at what I wrote to my son when he headed to college a few years ago:

## Relationships

*Journal Entry, July 27, 2006*

*As you are on this journey of discovery that I was talking to you about yesterday, remember to always ask yourself who is on this journey with you. Who is speaking into your life? Who is having an influence? Our travel companions make a real difference no matter who we are. Proverbs 13:20 comes to mind. "He who walks with the wise grows wise, but a companion of fools suffers harm."*

*Matthew 15:14b, "If a blind man leads a blind man, both will fall into a pit."*

*1 Corinthians 15:33, "Don't be misled: Bad company corrupts good character."*

*Remember, even if you are a leader, who you are with makes a difference. If your key friends are content to only have fun, to only be superficial, to waste days away pursuing nothing, it will have an impact.*

*In my first year of college, I was content to be around people who were not pursuing anything bigger than themselves. They pursued things and very seldom pushed themselves to be and do their best. They thought college life existed so that they could move from one party to the next. You know what? It had an impact as I slipped further and further into mediocrity.*

*Thank God something inside me was restless. Something said, "There has got to be more, something bigger and better to be a part of."*

*By the summer, I forced myself to get involved in Baptist Student Union (a Christian campus group). I took initiative to develop new relationships, to live with different people, to connect, have fun and be challenged in a different way.*

*Who I spent my time with had a tremendous impact on my life as I began to pursue God and find new ways to impact people. I was much more balanced in fun and discipline. In fact, it was because of those guys I learned the discipline of prayer, reading the Bible and memorizing Bible verses. I also had a blast going through life with people who are positive, people who push me to bigger things, people who are spontaneous and not rigid.*

*This still is important to me today. Are the people I've surrounded myself with having a positive impact? Are they going in a direction that I want to go? Are they taking me to a higher place or are they encouraging me to settle for mediocrity?*

*No matter where you are in life, keep asking those questions, because who we surround ourselves with makes a difference.*

Take a look around and find the people who will walk through life with you. It's hard work. The relationships may or may not last. There will be disappointments. Nevertheless, we cannot avoid the reality that we need those kinds of friends to move us forward on the journey.

## Friends Along the Way

Clearly, not all relationships develop into life-long friendships. Some people may walk a portion of our journey with us and then decide to take a different path. In reality, most will walk this kind of road. These relationships are valuable as well. God has used many friends in this manner to impact me in powerful ways during a particular season in my life. For several years, I had a group of friends that ventured with me to Crested Butte, Colorado. We mountain biked, fished, golfed and took part in other exciting adventures. Although a few of us still go today, some of those traditions ended when we all made adjustments due to life stages and other priorities. I must admit, I'm still a little sad about that. We had some great times together. I love those guys and miss them dearly, but the reality is — we don't invest in each other like we used to and that's okay.

I think my dad knew who his journey friends were and he had many friends along the way and invested accordingly. He also understood the value of connecting with his family—both the generations that came before him and those that followed after him. He always helped me remember that the connections we build with our families will often outlast our friendships and have a tremendous impact far beyond our lifetimes. Our biggest impact and greatest joys can come within the context of these relationships. More on this later.

## With Connections Come Disappointments

Whenever we enter into connections with other people, whether they are family or friends, we will deal with disappointments. When my wife and I were in our 20s, we shared life with a close group of three couples. The six of us played together, traveled, served and studied together. I thought these friendships would last a lifetime and, in many ways, they were some of the best times we ever had with friends and were some of the closest connections I'd ever experienced. But things changed. Some of the group went different directions, which was too bad for all of us. After all these years, I'm still deeply disappointed in how some of these relationships ended. It would be easy for me to conclude that relationships simply aren't worth the effort or heartache. I often wonder if I am better off not connecting with others in any kind of deep way. But if I go this route, I play right into the enemy's hand. By embracing the concept of the "Lone Ranger," I really become a lonely ranger, very vulnerable to the attacks of the enemy. Believe me, this has happened more than once in my life. The strategy of the enemy is to divide and conquer. It's not good for me to be alone and it's not healthy for my family to be on an island all by itself. I'm thankful for the deep connections we had and the opportunity to experience with that group, even if only for a season. When you experience the inevitable disappointment and disillusionment that just comes with relationships, do what it takes to get some resolution. Let it go and keep moving, take risks with other relationships. You're the only one who gets hurt by holding on to frustration and disappointment.

## Connecting to Places

Connecting is not just about people. We also need to stay connected to the places, activities and things that give us life and energy along the way. In the day-to-day busyness of work, in the economic pressures we face and in the time it takes to raise a family, many of us lose our life-filling, life-giving connections. Let's pause for a moment and see if we can reconnect a few of our loose wires. Remember the people, places and things that God has used to give you life, to encourage and energize you.

Over the course of your life, God has probably given you moments when you felt truly alive. You felt inspired, energized and ready to take on the world and fulfill your unique calling. Stop and ponder that for a bit. What were you doing at those moments? Where were you? Who was with you? Take time right now, carve out 30 minutes of quietness and journal what comes to mind. What are the activities or things that bring you energy and restore you? Discover those themes and make sure they are a regular part of your life.

For me, it's the mountains. It's hiking Trail 401 in Crested Butte, Colorado. It's biking at sunset and traveling with my family. It's the Sandhill Cranes migrating to central Nebraska. It's a morning at Summer Haven Lake. It's roller-blading or long boarding the boardwalk at Mission Beach, California. It's being in an April snowstorm with my wife in Estes Park, Colorado. It's a good laugh with my wife and some friends, a great concert, traveling with our kids, watching our youngest son catch his first white bass, walking the battlefields of Gettysburg with our daughter, who loves history like I do, and being in awe of the history and sacrifice at that place. All of those things are key connection times, places and memories that are absolutely critical in keeping me balanced, centered and purposeful.

## Connecting with Experiences

It's also Nebraska football. Ah, Nebraska football. If you're passionate about another team, then put its name here instead. Obviously, not all of us are sports fans, so if you're not one of those people, bear with me. To be a part of Husker football in the state of Nebraska is an amazing phenomenon. Husker football is an important connection for me. When I was little, the highlight of the fall season was driving the long road to Lincoln for a Husker football game. We were destined for a day of fun and excitement with dad and thousands of other people in the ever-so-famous sea of red. On other Saturdays during the fall harvest season, I remember listening to Husker football games on the radio in the tractor. We had to keep up with the action even though we couldn't be at the game in the stadium. Today, I still go to games with family and friends and I still love it. It's an escape. It's therapy. It's just plain fun.

Like the other thing I shared earlier, I see college football as a God kind of gift. Too often we have been made to feel guilty when we play, rest or engage in things we enjoy. We forget God created things for us to enjoy. He's given us permission and makes our hearts light up in certain situations. Look hard for these points of connection and, instead of feeling guilty like some would have you do, hang on to them and fight for them with all you've got.

One of my good friends comes alive when he rides his Harley. His eyes light up when he talks about the road trips that he and his friends have ventured on. He loves to show me pictures of his new bike and is always excited to share his plans for the next adventure. This is clearly a window into who he is, how he's wired and what he's looking for in life.

Be real for a moment and listen to the themes of your life. Think again—what are the things that excite you and fill you? What things give you substance, weightiness and strength? Find those places and activities that connect you at a deep level and make time for them in your life. If you don't, you will lose your way for sure. These things are critical for you to help mark your way. They're essential components on the map of your life.

Connections with people, places and experiences are all critical parts of the bigger connection that we were designed to be part of. God made us for relationship with Him and I am reminded again and again that the spiritual journey we are on is all about this relationship. It is the foundation of the spiritual experience. The life, death and resurrection of Jesus made a relationship with God possible. It's a life-changing connection with God that gives the rest of our lives purpose and hope. The things we love and are passionate about often give great insight into how He has designed us.

## Seeking that Connection with God

Pursuing that life-giving relationship with God takes intentionality. It takes a relentless commitment to take that next step and it takes unwavering belief that He does speak to you. Just the other day, I was reading, thinking and struggling with the idea of hearing God's voice and seeking His direction. I believe He still speaks, but we've got to find ways to listen.

In the first book of Samuel, there is a great conversation between Samuel and God. Samuel speaks with hope and an expectancy to hear from God. It's no different now. I believe He is ready to lead and direct you, but you need to keep pursuing Him and taking steps toward Him. Stay in conversation with God, and remember that He is not a "God of confusion, but of peace."

I find James 3:17 very important as well, "But the wisdom that comes from heaven is first of all pure; then peace-loving, considerate, submissive, full of mercy and good fruit, impartial and sincere." This verse has provided a great checklist as I have wrestled with various decisions along the road.

Trust your heart as God works through your desires, abilities and strengths. Surround yourself with others who have walked with God longer than you have. Gather wisdom from them and learn from their experiences. Be sure to weigh the advice you receive from others and make certain not to place too much or too little emphasis on another believer's insight. If you long to hear Him, make sure you carve out time to listen. Take regular time to be alone, to be quiet. This will be hard at first. Sometimes it will take hours, maybe overnight, but be silent. Wait for God to break through.

If you have those regular times of quiet, waiting on God and asking Him to direct you, I am confident He will do just that. And, as you move forward, make sure to seek some confirmation of direction from key people in your life. This is some of what has helped me through the years:

Remember key God moments in your life

Be alert to distractions that can take you away from your focus

Pray with expectancy and a hope that He will meet you

Commit to times of silence and solitude so you don't miss the sometimes quiet and assuring ways in which God speaks

Be fiercely committed to the people and things that breathe life into you

Pursue God with gumption

## Gumption

My grandfather often talked about gumption. To him, it was a stick-to-it-ness, the ability to hang in there no matter what comes your way.

When I was little, he would have me rake the leaves in his yard for one dollar. He would tell me to have gumption to finish the job, no matter how hard or how boring.

I knew he had gumption. He was married to my grandmother for more than 50 years before she died. Though the odds were against him, he stuck with farming through the Great Depression. Not only did he stick with it, he somehow made it profitable when so many others were failing. He was a faithful friend and father throughout his whole life. He lived with strength, compassion and grace. More importantly, he and my grandmother walked with God until their last days on earth. That doesn't mean they didn't struggle, doubt or ask questions, but they did endure. They hung in there, no matter what life threw at them.

My aunt and my dad would talk about their parents not merely praying a token prayer at meal time, but kneeling on the floor and thanking God for His provision each night before supper.

When I was little, I would often stay at their house. I would watch them go through a devotion and a short prayer every morning. Much of the discipline and passion to follow God came from my grandmother, who was relentless in her pursuit of God. The bottom line is — they had gumption about the things that were really important in their life.

When I think of gumption, a few things come to mind:

I think of a balance of passion and discipline. Isaiah 50:7 talks about setting our face like flint to do the will of God. It takes both passion and discipline to have staying power. We have to not only understand why something is important, but also be willing to do what it takes to keep those things important over the long haul.

Be alert to temptations and distractions that will get you off course whether it's procrastination, too many good opportunities, an inability to say no or a refusal to eliminate options. This used to be a real weakness of mine—I never wanted to close the door. Too often I would try to keep all possibilities open. Whatever it is for you, be aware of your blind spots.

Always be able to answer the question, "Why?" Those who have staying power, resolve, tenacity, gumption . . . they know why they do what they do and they remind themselves of that often.

My youngest has a dream to play college basketball. He is now a junior in high school and the why is what gets him through the hundreds of hours of off-season workouts and countless times at the gym. For him, it's not just performing, not just the love of basketball, it's more. It's a platform he feels will give him the opportunity to positively impact others. Yes, the why is critical.

Gumption requires others who will keep you encouraged, challenged and accountable. It requires someone in your life who won't let you settle or slip into mediocrity. If you looked at the times I've fallen back in my life, you could always see that I lacked people asking the hard questions. You would definitely see someone who was trying to do it alone.

We need to have this kind of gumption as we pursue things that bring us life. We have got to be relentless in our pursuit of others because, by nature, we resist close relationships and connections that bring deeper meaning to life.

Check out these words from a song by Green Day:

*I walk a lonely road*

*The only one that I have ever known,*

*Don't know where it goes,*

*But it's home to me and I walk alone . . .*

*Sometimes I wish someone out there will find me*

*'Til then I walk alone.*[2]

That can define the stories of too many people. Many things can lead us to this lonely walk—fierce independence, pride, hurt from past relationships, business, pain and disappointment in God or just the pace of life. Whatever the case, be determined and fiercely committed to staying connected to the people, events, experiences and things that bring you energy and life.

No matter how much of a risk it seems to be, staying where you're at is not an option. Resist the urge to play it safe, take the time now to do something you really love to do! Don't embrace the Lone Ranger. Take a risk and stay connected! Let others in! Don't take this journey alone!

STOP FOUR  -  REMEMBER THOSE NEAR

# REMEMBER THOSE NEAR

*In the busyness of life and the frantic pace of earning a living, chasing relationships, pursuing work and just living life, I don't want to miss it. I don't want to miss the hearts of those closest to me.*

Why is it so hard? Why is it so tough to save our best for those closest to us? I don't have any easy answers to that, but I was reminded of the importance of this again a few months ago.

I was living life at a frantic pace. Finding a rhythm to my life had been a struggle. In April, a friend called with the news that he had a couple of playoff tickets for a Lakers versus Nuggets game in Denver. Now, I'm no martyr -- I love basketball. I love watching it and playing it but, our son Dylan loves it more. The Lakers are his team. There was one problem. The only way I could pull it off was to drive the 15 hours up and back on the same day, driving virtually all night on the way home. Typically I would stretch the experience out, but I couldn't do it this time. I had many people call me crazy, but we decided to go for it. It was a great day! Watching him light up when the Lakers took the floor made it totally worth it. It was about much more than a basketball game. We had some great talks, a lot of fun and we made a fantastic memory that will last a long time!

On the long drive back, I was reminded of one of the great challenges in life and leadership:  that, in the busyness of life, in the frantic pace of earning a living, chasing relationships, pursuing work and just doing life, we make sure we don't miss it -- that we don't miss the hearts of those closest to us. It may take some adjustments and some significant personal sacrifice, but it's worth it every time.

To the best of my ability, knowing that many times I have fallen short, I want to do this well  and I want to encourage others to do the same.

Despite my passion around families, I have to admit that as a husband and a parent there are times I feel like I'm caught in an episode of that old TV show "Lost." Those characters were out on an island with an infinite amount of dangers. There were twists and turns to the plot and, every time you thought you knew what would happen next, you were probably wrong. My daughter and I watched that show whenever we could, and most of the time I felt lost (literally)! We were both unsure about where the story was going, always surprised by the progression of the show's plot and characters, perplexed by the choices certain characters made, and left confused and in the dark. For many of us, that's what family life sometimes feels like. However, unlike TV, where the characters come and go rather frequently, our family is with us for the long haul, regardless of the choices we make. Our families, whether good or bad, present or absent, have a profound impact on who we are and who we will become. While we can't change the past, we all have the opportunity to shape the family we are part of right now and set the course for future generations. What an amazing and overwhelming opportunity that is!

Family is an area I feel passionate about, perhaps because I've spent nearly three decades working with teens. I've seen the struggles facing the current generation of young people, partly because a large number of adults have opted out of family life. I saw this scenario in our son's high school basketball team, when only a few had any type of father figure at home. Those boys are not alone. They are some of the 24 million children growing up in America without their biological father at home and that does not come close to counting the many dads who have checked out or never checked in. In a national survey, over 70 percent of those surveyed said that "the physical absence of the father from the home is the most significant problem facing America."[1] Kids who grow up without fathers are more likely to be sexually promiscuous, abuse drugs and alcohol, commit delinquent acts and fail in school. Certainly it is not the only factor, as many single parents are doing an amazing job of raising their children, but it is a big factor and one that we can't ignore. So, dads and moms, we need to step up. We need to remember that we are, and will be, the most influential people in our kids' lives. It's not friends, the media, teachers or pastors. It is us! As the years pass, don't let yourself get passive; don't let yourself miss this. Our actions, or lack of actions, will have a profound impact on our family, our kids and the generations to follow.

Going a bit further, it's not just broken homes that produce broken children. Teens today say they need better communication with mom and more time with dad. Even parents who are physically present in the home are often absent in every other way. Too many of us leave our best somewhere else besides home. A few years ago, I attended a large conference for the organization where I was employed. This conference was held around the same time each year. It was important to be there. Our son was participating in an end-of-the-year basketball tournament for his junior varsity team, so I was leaving the meeting a couple of days early to get to the games. As I was walking out of the hotel, I ran into one of my peers who explained that he was making quite a sacrifice to be there and he was missing his son's last basketball game as a senior. I would not judge him; I have no doubt that he felt he was supposed to be at the meeting. I don't know all the circumstances of his life, but for me it seemed like an easy choice — go to the game.

I left the hotel that day with a new resolve to get it right and to help others do the same. I'm putting forth my best efforts to hold on to small windows or opportunities. I don't want to miss precious moments with my family because I thought there were more important things to do. We give our prime time — hours, days and our prime years — to the job, the ministry or other urgent demands, and our families are often left wanting something more, longing to have just a little bit of the energy and passion we poured into other things. We need to rearrange our lives so we give our best to what will last the longest — our family relationships.

## Life is Great When a Family is at its Best

I'm very passionate about families, not simply because I've seen what so often goes wrong, but because I've experienced what happens when family works the way it should. One of the most vivid memories of my dad was his presence at a little league baseball game in early summer of my fifth-grade year. It was time to harvest wheat. For a farmer, there are many urgent times, but wheat harvest could be the most pressing. If storms blow through, the crop can be lost and there is a very small window to bring in the crop. Everyone is in the field 24/7 during the harvest. Well, almost everyone. I will always remember heading to the plate, knowing that I would probably strike out again, glancing over at the crowd, all of 40 people, and realizing there was only one man in the stands. Everyone else had to work, but one man knew it wouldn't be the end of the world if he took off an hour, even if it was harvest time. After yet another strikeout, he told me to keep swinging! I didn't fully grasp the impact of that night until later in life, but it changed me and helped shape me into the father I wanted to be. In his mind, I'm sure he had no idea the level of impact that one night would have. He made it to many games, but that particular night, one man in the stands made a difference.

I had a mom and dad who made their marriage and relationship with me and my two sisters an absolute priority. My parents took the time to invest in us even during the busiest seasons of their lives. My mom devoted many of her best years to serving us, as well as many others. Our meals, our home and our memories centered on the stable core that she helped provide. She relentlessly served and rarely became too focused on her tasks and to-do lists. She was the one who took a mattress out into the yard when I was eight and camped out with me. As we looked at the stars in the vast Nebraska sky, I felt challenged to dream big. My parents didn't know that they would both die very young (Dad at 59 and Mom at 62). Nevertheless, they didn't put off the most important priority—investing time in their family. If they had waited until they had more time, until they simplified their lives or slowed down, it would have never happened.

My grandpa taught my dad that taking time for family is important, even if it doesn't always make sense. In the middle of the Great Depression, my grandma and grandpa did what must have appeared to be foolish to their friends and neighbors. While everyone around them lived in fear of the crumbling economy and the devastating drought, these two risk-takers loaded up the kids, asked friends to watch the farm and headed out for a vacation. My grandfather knew the years were going quickly and he needed to forge some family memories. For two weeks they drove west to see the Grand Canyon, San Diego, the coast and San Francisco; then they headed home through the Rockies. When everyone else was tightening up and not risking anything, he was investing in farming, yes, but also in his family. Others were selling but he was finding ways to buy what mattered most. They did it again in 1939. They went to Washington, D.C., New York City and the East Coast. These trips opened up the world to their kids and left a legacy in our family of spending extended times together, no matter what the cost.

For many of you, this is a critical fork in the road. You don't have this kind of legacy. If your family has either let you down or never been there for you, you need to know this: there is hope. In no way should your struggles or wounds be diminished. You needed a family to nourish and support you and, for whatever reason, it didn't happen; but, that is not the end of the story. Let me tell you about two of my friends, Kyle and Ben.

When Kyle's mom found out she was pregnant, Kyle's dad insisted she have an abortion. They already had too many kids. On the way to the abortion clinic, Kyle's mom stood up to her husband and said she would not abort her baby. Her husband pushed her out of the car and drove away. He never saw his wife or kids again. He never met his yet-to-be-born son Kyle. Imagine the rejection and feelings of abandonment Kyle has wrestled with.

Ben's story begins differently, but ends up in a similar place. His parents were missionaries who later returned to the United States to be in full-time ministry. Somewhere along the way, Ben's dad lost his way and left his mom and four kids. Years later, the personal, relational and spiritual wounds are still deep. Ben has many questions that don't have simple answers. In fact, there will never be an answer that is sufficient.

Both Kyle and Ben have determined to do life differently. They each have continued to pursue God and the fulfillment that only He can bring. Kyle is now the father of four boys. He longs to be a great dad even though he never experienced firsthand what that looks like. Kyle is starting to invest in each of his kids in a deep way and is raising four young warriors. But, like all parents, he will need others to help him remember not to get lost in his work, to remember that these are the most important relationships he will ever have. Like all who have been wounded or abandoned by family, Kyle and Ben have the opportunity to write a new chapter in their family history. They have the opportunity to be pioneers, of sorts, and chart a new course for their marriages, children, grandchildren and their children's grandchildren.

You can forge a new path in your family's story as well. You can choose to intentionally invest your best at home—in the people you live with and interact with everyday. Those of us who have been blessed with a strong family legacy have to determine now not to coast and make sacrificial choices in order for things to work. We have to choose to invest deeply in our family and not take them for granted. I often struggle with making that choice on a daily basis as this journal entry reflects:

*Journal Entry, November 12, 2004,*

*Help me Lord, to be more engaged with my own kids – more intentional. Help me not to take out frustrations of the day on them. Help me leave a legacy of balance and positive affirmation, not harshness. Help me let them know how much I believe in them, how much I know that they've got what it takes. Help me show Drew and Dylan how to treat women by being a better model when interacting with Marcia, by honoring and respecting her. Help them forget the times I've screwed this up.*

*I don't have long with Drew. Give me teachable moments. Allow me to stop focusing on work and myself and seize the moments with my kids. Help me instill in them faith, honor, strength of character and an understanding of what is important in life.*

*In family, work, in transition to something else and in my relationship with God, help me not to be a passive spectator but rather an engaged participant in the journey.*

## The Foundation of Family

The marriage relationship is the foundation of family. For those of you who are married, this has to be the starting point. Too many parents place their focus on their children and neglect the relationship with their spouse, leading to a decline in the marriage. I was guilty of that, and Marcia and I were slowly drifting apart. Unintentionally, everything else became a priority except our relationship. My focus became myself, our kids, having fun, finances and work, just about everything but my relationship with my wife and that trend put us at risk. In the long run, kids do far better when mom and dad take time to invest in each other and the marriage relationship. I have to remind myself often that the most important modeling I can do for our kids is having the right kind of relationship with my wife. We have tried our best to have a balanced relationship of fun, activity and depth. More than ever, we strive now to demonstrate this kind of healthy, balanced relationship because it is vital for our children and it is needed and critical for us as well. In the maze of business, ministry and family, this requires a very intentional effort. Though I've tried my hardest to make my wife a priority, many times I've failed miserably, but I'll keep trying. We still schedule time for regular dates and an occasional weekend get-away in order to focus on our relationship. Periodically, I have to look at my calendar to see what my schedule says about the priority of my marriage.

Not only do Marcia and I model our marriage relationship before our kids, but we also decided early on that we would live authentically before our kids. We try to let our kids see us work through conflict, reach resolution and show forgiveness; and they have had a lot of opportunity to see me say, "I'm sorry." Kids need to learn that conflict is a normal part of relationships and that resolution is possible. Too many parents show kids conflict without the resolution. Hopefully, we have shown them more of the latter.

I will never have a more difficult, more rewarding, more emotionally charged or more important job than the job of being a parent. Strategic parents are still the primary influence in their children's lives. Don't let your emotions or anyone tell you otherwise. Despite how it sometimes feels, parents are the primary influence in the lives of their kids. It is not their music, their friends, their pastor or coach — it's you!

I really want to know our kids. I want to discover how God has gifted them. I want to recognize, affirm and celebrate the unique person that He has created and help them figure out why God designed him or her just that way. I want to know what fills our daughter's soul and what makes our sons laugh. I want to lavish love on our children by really listening to them, sharing and investing in their interests and helping them hone their unique abilities. At the end of the day, I want my children to feel like I'm on their team, not on their backs.

That kind of relationship takes time. We've got to relentlessly pursue our children and take all the time necessary to build a relationship with them. It's easy to say that parents should spend time with their children, but what does that look like? I have made four types of time commitments to our kids. These may or may not work for you, so use them as starting points to find what fits your family.

I try to do my best to:

Remember that relationships have to be a priority. With all the difficult stuff that our kids can face, I have to fight to keep the relationship strong.

Take time to discover and develop their unique strengths and interests.

Be intentional and live each season of life with no regrets.

Embrace and celebrate threshold moments in our family and the lives of our kids.

Constantly ask the key questions about my family life. What does my family need most right now? What do I want my legacy to be? Am I storing up a treasure chest of memories for our children?

## Day-to-Day Interaction

I want to be intentional about investing in my family every day. Many of life's lessons are learned along the way. I want to be in close enough proximity to our kids, emotionally, relationally and physically, that they are able to easily see and pick up on these lessons that are tucked into our everyday life.

I watched my father embrace the reality of his ruined fields and witnessed the everyday relationship that he had with God. I saw him deal with the ups and downs, the frustrations, doubts and victories that each day brought.

On the day of the hailstorm, it was not what he said at that particular point in time, but it was what he modeled that was most important. It wasn't significant to see him go to church the next Sunday. It was important that I saw him have church that night in the middle of a flattened cornfield—just him, God and a good friend who came and stood by his side.

As best I can, I want to invite my family into my day-to-day journey. Back when our kids were younger, I took them with me to work and ministry events as much as I could. It was critical for them to see all (well, most) of my daily life: its doubts, questions, struggles, victories, the mundane and the exciting. Inviting my family into my daily routine was also an added source of accountability. I want to share in the day-to-day lives of our kids. To have any shot at that, I have to be intentional with the way I spend my time every single day.

## The Uniqueness of Each Family Member

No two children are identical. We have a creative God to thank for that. As parents, one of our jobs is to help our children discover and embrace their unique strengths and interests—even if it takes us outside our comfort zone.

In the movie "Remember the Titans," Coach Boone, the new coach in town, has the following encounter with the young daughter of one of his assistants:

**Sheryl Yoast:** *Coach Boone, you did a good job up here. You ran a tough camp from what I can see.*

**Coach Boone:** *Well I'm very happy to have the approval of a five-year old.*

**Sheryl Yoast:** *I'm nine and a half, thank you very much.*

**Coach Boone:** *Why don't you get this little girl some pretty dolls or something, coach?*

**Coach Yoast:** *I've tried. She loves football.*[2]

Sheryl Yoast did indeed love football and her father encouraged her interest even when others felt he should push her toward more "appropriate" interests. We have to be students of our children. What do they gravitate toward? What are they good at? What makes them smile? Companies like Gallup have made a living at connecting people to their strengths. We should learn something from these companies that do it so well. We should help our kids identify their strengths and do whatever we need to do to help them embrace those strengths.

I would encourage you to spend individual time with your kids, focused on their interests, not yours. If your son is a musician and you were a quarterback, put away the football and pick up the guitar. If your daughter loves nature, but your idea of a good hike is walking around the pool at the nearest Marriott, check out of the hotel and go camping. Our kids will look forward to spending one-on-one time with us when it is about what they like to do. One of the greatest gifts my father gave me was not only his permission but also his blessing to be who God uniquely made me.

## No Regrets

This is a point of self-evaluation. We must take time to look at how we live our lives and ask some important questions:

Would my spouse and kids say that they are a priority to me, as much as I would say they are a priority?

Am I intentionally investing in my family? Am I investing in each member individually?

Even though I've made mistakes and would do some things differently, from this day forward, will I make choices today that will allow me to live this season of life with no regrets?

What are the unique interests and abilities of my spouse and kids?

Am I nurturing and encouraging them to pursue their passions?

As a single person, what do I need to adjust and change, think about or pray toward that will help me be ready if God does give me a family? Do I struggle with setting healthy boundaries around me?

Take time to regularly ask yourself the hard questions. Invite others to ask you as well. Time is of the essence and our days are far too precious to waste simply because we didn't periodically take time to evaluate our lives.

## Threshold Moments

Several years ago, Marcia and I decided that we wanted to take advantage of significant life thresholds to pass on some things to our children, as well as celebrate important moments. We decided that each threshold would be marked with a ceremony of sorts, a unique experience designed for each child. Each event had a spiritual element and provided important reference points or life markers. Much of our thinking on these threshold events was shaped by the book, "Raising a Modern Day Knight"[3] by Robert Lewis, a book we highly recommend.

We chose to mark these thresholds with each of our children:

The summer before first grade

The transition to middle elementary (third or fourth grade)

The start of seventh grade and the teen years

Their 16<sup>th</sup> birthday

Graduation

College

We are still approaching these thresholds with our youngest, but let me tell you how we marked these moments with our oldest, just because we've already passed through these significant stages with him. Before he started first grade, I took Drew to a Kansas City Chiefs football game. We saw Joe Montana in one of his last games as an NFL quarterback. We had some pretty good talks about what Drew would face when he started "full-time school."

In Drew's fourth-grade year, I surprised him and took him out of school. I gave his teacher a note that said, "I appreciate you teaching my son but, for the next couple of days, I want to talk with him about God, friends and the unique issues of upper elementary." We went to Phoenix to watch the Nebraska-Arizona State football game. Nebraska was the defending national champion but got shut out 19-0. We experienced a memorable defeat, ate a big slice of humble pie as we walked out of that stadium and had some great talks as we hiked in the hills around Phoenix.

The seventh-grade trip was all about the emergence of adolescence, the upcoming teen years and all the unique changes and pressures that were coming Drew's way. I wanted us to listen together to a couple of CDs on peer pressure, understanding sex and developing convictions in tough situations. I knew the only way to do that was to trap Drew in the car on the way to a fun event, so we drove to the Big 12 basketball tournament in Kansas City. We saw seven basketball games in three days, ate well, had a lot of fun and listened to the CDs and talked about them on the way there and back.

When Drew was 14, we took his "coming of age trip." I let our children choose where we go on this trip. Drew wanted to go fishing so we headed to British Columbia to fish for king salmon. Everything was great except that we didn't catch any fish. As we headed toward our third and last day, I prayed, "God, I don't know if you really care about fishing. I don't know if it matters in the big picture of life whether we catch any fish or not. There are a lot of critical things going on in the world right now, but to my 14-year-old son, this is pretty important. In fact, for him and me right now, this is huge. I just want to pray for us to be able to catch some fish, lead our guide to the right spot. It would make this memory so much richer." Well, that night we caught our limit of king salmon. Two of them were over 16 pounds. It was incredible.

I know there are many more crucial issues to care about. I struggle with why God seems to answer one prayer and not another. I struggle with why He often seems quiet, detached and uninvolved in our everyday lives. I am not saying it will happen like that; maybe that was just a random thing. All that I know is, on that night in a little boat, on the edge of the North American continent, looking out over the vast Pacific Ocean, God gave us a little glimpse of heaven — a window into His abundance, a blessing and a memory that, for father and son, will last a lifetime.

One of our talks on the trip was about King Josiah. At that time, it was obvious to me that Drew had a gift for leadership, an ability to motivate, inspire and mobilize others. I wanted him to know that age doesn't restrict, impact or hold us back from accomplishing great things. This was just one of the great talks we had because I was intentional about making some memories and celebrating the stages with him. You can do the same for your children whether you take them to British Columbia or the creek a mile from your house.

Our daughter, Ali, picked a history trip to Gettysburg, Pennsylvania, where we stayed in a 250-year-old bed and breakfast inn. We had great talks and were in constant awe of the stories of strength, courage, sacrifice and love in Gettysburg. Perhaps the most memorable event of the trip with our daughter happened on the first night. We decided to take a "ghost walk" through the town. They told many "factual" and fictional stories as we walked around the town. Toward the end of the tour, we came out in front of the lodge where we were staying. The guide asked us to look up to the second level and focus on the second room from the end. She explained how that room was the Meade Suite and was, in fact, the most haunted room in Gettysburg. Our eyes widened and our mouths dropped to the ground – that was the room we were in! When we got back to the room, I looked under the bed more than once. I was the one that got "spooked." We laugh about this often. It's a memory we will share as long we live. Was it worth the time, money and effort? A resounding YES! You can't afford to miss those types of moments.

At age 16, we presented all three kids with a journal of letters from people who had invested in their lives. A cousin sent a letter that included "the 16 things I wish an older cousin would have told me." These letters are priceless. They speak volumes of truth about who our kids are. They challenge them, inspire them and help them to envision an amazing future. If they ever doubt that they have a whole team of raving fans on their side, all they have to do is take out their journal and read those letters.

When Drew turned 18, we had a cigar and a great talk with one of my best friends. Celebrating his next step toward manhood seemed right. Sometimes, the most spiritual thing I can do is not to sit down and have a quiet time or a devotional. Sometimes, the most spiritual thing I can do is have that cigar and talk with my son and encourage him to keep reaching for things that are bigger than he is. Tell him to keep pursuing—moving toward God.

I have made similar commitments to mark threshold events with each of our kids. The point isn't how expensive or extravagant the experience will be, but you do want to make it memorable, intentional and inspirational. Find stages you want to embrace—celebrate in a way that fits your family. Invite others to be a part of this. The simple things are sometimes the best.

The older two are off to college and jobs, forging their own way. We still have our youngest at home to experiment on! I hope the relationship we've relentlessly pursued will see us through. I hope that we will continue to share rich experiences in the years ahead.

My dad died just a few days before he and I were scheduled to leave on a deep-sea fishing trip. Even up to the end of his life, he was planning more creative experiences.

I want to be like that. I want to invest where it matters most. I don't always get it right, but I want to keep trying. One night during Drew's senior year of high school, we had a conflict. Right in the middle of our disagreement, I asked Drew, "Well, how would you parent your kids in this situation?" Drew said, "I will parent my kids like you guys have done it." That's a pretty high compliment and a very daunting challenge—one that should put the fear of God in every parent.

*Journal Entry, May 23, 2001*

*Lord, to the best of my ability, with the unique strengths and weaknesses I bring, help me to do the best I can. Help me remember it's not just about the destination, it's about the journey. In fact, with our kids, it may be totally about the journey. Help me be intentional with the day-to-day. Help me do the best I can. To invest in the relationships that matter most. To invest well in such a way that it will positively impact them and those they encounter throughout their lives. Help me not to hold them too close. Help me to encourage them to pursue, discover and embrace who they truly are. With all my faults, knowing I've made mistakes, knowing I can't change the past, help me come alongside my family in deep real ways. Show me ways to enjoy them and have fun. And help me do the best I can at ushering them into the next season of their lives.*

In the journey we are on together throughout this book, this is a critical stopping place. This is an important time to evaluate, anticipate and decide what kind of parent you want to be. No matter how old or young you may be, whether you are married or single, you have a chance now to decide what kind of difference you will make in your family, whether that's now or sometime in the future.

What will be your mark or the legacy you will leave for your family? Are you being intentional, day to day, with the people that matter most? Do you have a plan, a road map for how you want to embrace, experience, empower and celebrate the time you've been given with your family? Whether you are down the road a bit already, just beginning, or single and thinking about the years ahead, now is the time to make things happen. Now is the time to relentlessly pursue the relationships closest to you and set the pace, chart the course, make the map. One way or another, you will leave your mark on their lives. Decide now what you want that to look like.

STOP FIVE   -   EMBRACE THE MYSTERY

# EMBRACE THE MYSTERY

*God's calling is not a place, not a position. It is the theme and rhythm of your life. To find that rhythm, to understand how God has already spoken into your life is the challenge and the opportunity that awaits you.*

How, and for what, has God uniquely designed me? In this season of life, what is the passion and mission that drives me? What is so compelling to me that I just can't let it go? In my 20s and contemplating a career move, pastor and author Calvin Miller once told me that life has a certain rhythm to it. The key to a life of impact is finding that particular rhythm and staying within it. That imagery has never left me.

When we talk about navigating through this crazy life adventure, it is critical that we pause on the journey and address the concept of our "calling." Webster defines calling as a "strong inner impulse toward a particular course of action, especially when accompanied by conviction of divine influence."[1] You know, that pretty much nails it! I like to look at calling as that unique mark, a unique pull that God has placed on your life. Calling, it seems, is what He has designed, equipped and prepared us for. Calling isn't something you are paid to do. It is more about the essense of who you are—a combination of the themes, passions, values and experiences of your life.

## What is My Calling?

Do you really believe that you were not created by random chance, but with a purpose and a mission, and that what you uniquely bring to the table is critical to the bigger story? Over and over again, the Bible tells us that God has a plan for us. He tells us that He knows us inside and out and knew all about us even before we were born (Psalm 139:15-16). He tells us that we can count on Him in any circumstance (Jeremiah 33:3). He directs the lives of His creation (Job 12:10). He tells us that He will show us the way we should go (Psalm 32:8 and Isaiah 45:2-3). So why is the quest to find and fulfill our calling so often frustrating and confusing? Why do we often feel lost? If God really does have a plan for us, why is it so elusive, so mysterious?

For one thing, I think we miss the essence of calling. Calling is not a place, job or a position. It is a sense of knowing and embracing what I have done throughout my life. It utilizes the unique ways God has gifted me. It is not a destination we will clearly arrive at one day. It really is a rhythm and a flow to life that we must constantly try to find and stay within. Why doesn't God just lay it all out in front of us? I referred to this earlier in my journal ... I think it is because deciphering the mystery of our lives keeps us seeking Him. If He simply handed us a life map with our direction marked with a big X, we'd most likely walk away from Him and head off to fulfill our destiny. By unveiling one thing at a time, by retaining the great mystery of our lives, God causes us to keep pursuing Him and, in reality, that might be the whole point.

Another reason calling is so hard to get a handle on is that it is different for every single one of us. Your cal ling may be similar to someone else's, but it is not identical. My father and I had different callings and one of the greatest gifts he ever gave me was permission to not follow in his footsteps. He was a third generation farmer and

I was the only son — the natural one to carry on the family business. However, I knew early on that it just wasn't for me. I did not have farming in my DNA.

My dad had a dream of having a family cabin on the lake—a place where the family could gather to play, ski, swim, laugh and rest—a place that would be a connecting point for the family in the future. He found the perfect lot at Summer Haven Lake near Kearney, Nebraska. Our own children know the place well. We've spent hundreds of hours there with friends and family. The cabin is a special place with a huge picture window that looks over the lake, some large cottonwood trees and a nice sandy beach. We've made plenty of great memories there.

We are blessed by the fact that my dad fulfilled one part of his calling. That's the way calling works. When we do what God designed us to do, it blesses those around us. When we live out the passions and desires that have been placed in our hearts, amazing things — supernatural things — happen. Our words and actions have impact far beyond what we can imagine. It shouldn't surprise us when things just feel right, when we sense we are going to a whole different level. When we do what He made us to do, we are like a finely tuned engine, hitting on all cylinders. Work gets done. People go places. Things happen. We feel at peace. We have a sense of rhythm.

My dad was a great example. He built that cabin in 1971 and more than 40 years later, we still go there in the summer. It is still a place that draws extended family together, even though our parents are no longer living. His dream for that cabin, and its impact of drawing family and friends together, has outlived him and I hope it, or something similar, will outlive me as well.

### Clues to Your Calling

So how in the world do you begin to discover your calling? What road markers have you been given for this quest? A friend told me over lunch one day that there are some things he looks for in regards to calling; we must identify those things that awaken us, deepen us and fulfill us. That is a great perspective. I look for common themes and trends throughout my life. If I were to chart out the highs and lows of each season of my life, what would I find? If I were to think through the key turning-point moments in my life, what were they? More importantly, what were the messages, the themes, the clues that God was speaking to me?

Do this: list your most significant moments in the past 10 years, five years, and the last year. Once you've done that, invite others to listen to your story. Have them look for common themes and messages that your life is speaking to you. I believe you'll gain valuable insight into what the next years of your life should look like. The best road map is to remember and listen to your own life.

## Remember

We've all had moments when our hearts just seemed to come alive, moments when we felt an eternal tug at our hearts, inspiring us and making us want to be more. Those moments help us begin to identify and connect with our passions, strengths, talents and calling. We don't want to miss them. Look for and remember times when you got excited and felt ready to pursue something with passion. Remember what you were doing when you really felt alive, when you felt yourself go to a whole different level. Remember those times when you've done something that seemed easy, maybe even effortless, and others have affirmed your strengths, talents and abilities. Remember and write those things down! Ponder them, study them, and look for any themes that begin to emerge.

Remembering some of the ways God has uniquely spoken to you can happen in a moment or it can unfold more slowly, like the chapter of a book. It can happen through an image, a song, a passage from a book or a random conversation. Insight could come through journaling, movies, friends or something in nature. God will use many different things to communicate truth to you about your calling. Keep your eyes and ears open.

Many times we will have those awakening experiences when we are young. In his book, "Windows of the Soul," Ken Gire says, "There are certain doors in our childhood that open and let the future in."[2]

I can see this in my own life. Special times with my family and friends woke up something inside of me. I also know that I was an initiator even at a young age. I was always the one organizing fun things to do, getting people together, tracking the memories. It's as if I was compelled to create meaningful experiences, ensuring that no one would forget them! I felt energized when I was doing those things. God was speaking to me in some way. In an earlier chapter, I spoke about my third-grade experience relating to the movie, "To Sir, with Love." This was the stop in a journey that clearly showed me that I am made to be involved in the unconventional transformation of people's lives. Throughout my life, this has been confirmed again and again.

Our oldest son had some experiences that clarified his calling through athletics. We saw him come alive when he had a chance to compete and be part of a team. When he was in third grade, his basketball team lost a big game. Two days later, he was still talking about that game. His mom told him to keep it in perspective. It was, after all, a third-grade basketball game. Drew looked at her earnestly and said, "Mom, you don't get it. I about died that day." That moment was a window into who Drew is. He has an intense desire to compete and win. I suspect that is part of his calling. His passion and his ability to connect with people are both compelling and contagious. He gravitates toward the place of influence. He wants to be on a big stage. He has a lot of questions and wonders now what he should be giving his life to. I have no doubt that we will see God develop and use these things in his life.

Our daughter loves working with kids. Her heart seems to come alive whenever she has a chance to work with underprivileged children. On a recent mission trip, children seemed to flock to her. She is also the one her friends constantly come to when they need to work through a problem. In many ways, she has served as a counselor to many people. Both of these are insights into her future calling and, no matter what her future job may be, she will always be able to embrace this deeper sense of who she is and what her life should be about.

Our youngest has tremendous compassion for people, for animals, for the things God has created. He is deeply moved by peoples' stories, and leads by his actions more than his words. God is using his talents to influence many and show them they can make good choices and do things the right way. These are great insights into who my kids are and who God has created them to be.

How do you know when one of these clarifying moments is a God thing? Maybe it's because inspiration comes with it. You can't seem to let go of the passion and creative energy that comes with it. Maybe it's just a sense of God's leading. Maybe it's because you're affirmed by those around you. Either way, get yourself to a place where you can clear your mind and remember. It is a key to unlocking the mystery of your life and where you are going next.

**Listen**

Having a rhythm to our life will touch the deepest part of who we are. When we walk with God and practice listening, we will begin to discern, at a deeper level, what we have been designed to do. I believe our life map is partially found in our desires. What do you long to do? What would you be a part of if there were no economic obstacles?

What would you do if it did not matter if you failed?

I've looked back through my journals for insight into my own desires. Below are some questions I've heard from others and have often asked myself. Maybe you'll find them useful as you begin to look deep into your own heart:

> What does my heart need right now to get refreshed, recharged and refocused?
>
> Where is God at work?
>
> How can I use my gifts to uniquely contribute? Where are my leverage points?
>
> What needs to be done and what can I do about it?
>
> If there were no boundaries, if I wasn't afraid of any roadblocks, what would I try to do?
>
> Am I walking by fear or faith? Fear makes me a prisoner, faith sets me free.
>
> What have significant people in my life told me about my strengths and abilities?
>
> When do I feel my life has a real rhythm?

After spending some extended time alone wrestling with these questions, I wrote the following about the desires of my soul, about my calling:

*Journal Entry, February 15, 2005*

*I'm further down the road of discovery than I think. Keep the fire burning, and help me Lord to enjoy the journey, to enjoy life. The time for feeling down, defeated, feeling like I'm going nowhere, needs to end. The time has come to take bold steps, be persistent and follow through on what God has told me. The time is here to come alongside young men and to challenge the 30- and 40-somethings and help them engage and invest in their families. It's time for me to boldly live out the themes of my family and personal life.*

*To encourage young leaders to follow their dreams.*

*To help men and families band together.*

*To call them to a bigger story and higher purpose.*

*To help them discover their rhythm, to leave a legacy and begin to understand what it means to finish well.*

*To help them find ways to enjoy and celebrate the journey.*

These are my deepest desires. As I understand it, this is my calling at this point in my life, and this has been confirmed in countless ways that I could live out this calling through a variety of jobs, contexts, opportunities and places. God has probably not revealed the whole picture to me yet and that's what keeps me pursuing Him wholeheartedly. Your desire will look different. It will be as unique and individual as you are, but it will stir the passions and take you deeper into the heart of God. So remember to listen, slow down, create margin and listen some more. It will take practice—it is hard work! Nevertheless, I believe you will be amazed at what you will hear.

## Space and Pace

How hard is it for you to unplug and step away from the crazy pace we often find ourselves in? What does it take for you to pull away from the noise, the busyness and create space in your life to really listen?

Where do you need to go to help you get the right pace to your life? For me, it's Trail 401 in Crested Butte, Colorado. The pressures, worries and questions seem to melt away there. The truth is, if I don't find a way to get to "Trail 401" on a regular basis, if I don't create some space and pace in my life, I will die spiritually. Getting away is not a new phenomenon, of course. Jesus did it many times. In Matthew 14:23; 15:29, Mark 6:45–46 and Luke 5:15–16, Jesus goes to the mountain. He goes to the place of solitude, refuge and beauty. He created the space in His life which, I suspect, helped give Him the strength He needed to step out every day.

When the time is right, God will take us places, give us opportunities and put us around people who help bring fulfillment and understanding to who we are and what we were created to do. When we live out our calling, we will experience a deep satisfaction and a rhythm to our life that is hard to put into words, but we have to be willing to step into it and do what it takes to stay there.

In your life, if you're in a place where you're feeling restless or unfulfilled, then I am excited for you! God may be trying to stir things up. He may be moving you toward something special. There is a scene in "The Breakfast Club," a great movie about high school kids in the '80s. In this particular scene, the kids are talking about their parents. One of the girls says that, "Adults have given up. They are content to go through the motions, work, get their stuff ... they've just lost heart."[3]

Those adults have lost pursuit of their calling. They have forgotten that, young or old, God wants to do great things through us. They forgot that, to not lose heart, they will be required to step out from the comfortable, the safe and the predictable. If we're lacking a sense of fulfillment and purpose, it might be because we stopped taking risks and stopped pursing life as an adventure.

I think there is a large myth that exists with the concept of calling; believing that when you discover your calling you will live in a constant state of fulfillment. That is not an accurate picture of what it means to live in our calling. In reality, there are moments of remembering and listening, when we catch a glimpse of how God is using us and working His plan, but they are surrounded by many ordinary, restless days. I think back to a devotional I read a long time ago, written by an extraordinary Christian author, Oswald Chambers who said something like, "We must learn to live in the ordinary gray day according to what we saw on the mountain!"[4]

That's a great challenge to me, especially since many of my moments of remembering and recognizing my calling have occurred in the Colorado Rockies. How can I live life with a sense of calling and purpose? How can I stay passionate and balanced in the ordinary, mundane day-to-day, yet stay focused on the sense of calling that was captured in the mountains?

I love the mountains. For some reason, I think more clearly there. Earlier I mentioned Trail 401 and, for many years, I have biked down that trail in Crested Butte, Colorado. Right above Gothic Pass, you have to push your bike up this single-track trail. After an aggressive stretch through a meadow, you emerge through some trees and you can see the trail wind down below, through the bowl at the top of the mountain. You can see for miles down the valley to Crested Butte. On the other side, if you climb a little higher, you can see the Maroon Bells.

I have had many great moments with friends and with God at the top of that trail. I came to somewhat of a peace with the loss of my parents there. I have caught ideas and thoughts up there regarding my future and often, for whatever reason, I just feel closer to God and more in His presence on that mountaintop.

The trail winds through open rock fields as it descends from above timberline, through aspen forests, creeks and springs, through abandoned cabins and meadows of wild flowers. You ride through a stream and weave around dense pine forests. Some of the real beauty is grown down in the valley, but the view from up high is hard to beat.

Then, there is the time to unwind in Crested Butte, to connect with friends over nachos and a beer, to meet new people and remember that every person has a story they need to share. Determining how to bring back the energy and clarity I get there is always a challenge, but it is critical because, for now, I still live my life, day-to-day, in the flatlands. I have to remind myself often about the whispers of God in the mountains. I must remember those times when God woke me up and took me to a different place, and you have to as well. You will eventually fade or spiritually die if you lose sight of those mountaintops. Decide now that you will do whatever it takes to create the space and find the pace you need to focus on what God is calling you into.

## It is All in the Timing

Another tricky thing about calling is the whole issue of timing. Habakkuk 2:3 says, "For the revelation awaits an appointed time; it speaks of the end and will not prove false. Though it linger, wait for it; it will certainly come and will not delay."

If you feel that God told you something about your calling, hold on to it. Don't let it go. Sometimes, for whatever reason, we just have to wait. It may seem like an incredibly long time of silence; you may even feel like quitting or giving up. During these times, we should keep moving toward our calling as best we can, stand watch and be ready so that we can move ahead full throttle when the time comes.

Several years ago, I had a dream (a literal dream) of developing a ministry for young emerging leaders and hurting ministry leaders. I began to take steps, to cast a vision, create a business plan, meet with people, seek funding and get training. These were all the right things to do, yet when it came time to take the step of faith and launch Harbor

Ministries, the message seemed clear: "Not yet." I kept searching, thinking through new ideas, new angles, new training, but still, the message was, "Not yet." Now, several years after this calling first came to me, I have launched this new ministry. It took years of waiting, a willingness to surrender and some extended times in the wilderness. God had some significant work to do in my own life that wasn't easy, but was totally necessary to get me ready for this mission. I went through a time of deep brokenness, but I emerged from this very dark time in a much better place to lead. I had to be willing to wait, keeping watch over the vision and readying myself for the right time. Did I get discouraged? Absolutely, but I had to remember what I sensed God telling me in those "higher moments."

> "See, I am doing a new thing! Now it springs up; do you not perceive it? I am making a way in the desert and streams in the wasteland." Isaiah 43:19

Clarity comes when I remember that God wanted to use me to do something different, something that could transform the lives of leaders. Even though it took years, the timing came and there really was a sense of rhythm to it. It was a long wait, but now it seems right and I have no choice but to step into it.

In the years ahead, you will be used in some unique and powerful ways and your passions, desires and talents are keys to the discovery. Clarity will come for you as you remember to listen and look for the common themes in your life.

## Will You Dare?

Nothing compares to the joy and satisfaction of living out your part in the bigger story. Nothing. I dare you to ask God to awaken His calling in your life. I challenge you to clear a day each month in your schedule, take a notebook and get away by yourself at a place where you won't be distracted. Again, ask yourself some key questions.

What are some of the themes God has put in your life?

What do you find yourself doing without thinking?

What are you gravitating toward?

What do you just plain love?

What things, when you do them, take you to another level of awareness, joy and fulfillment?

Over the past several years, what are the four or five most meaningful experiences you've been a part of?

Divide your life into three sections: childhood, high school and adulthood. For each era of your life, write down your most powerful memories, events and successes. Get it all down in front of you and ask God to show you the themes that begin to emerge. Set up a personal planning retreat and commit to this kind of retreat once a year. Don't be afraid to invest in this area of your life. If you'd like another resource on this, check out Tom Paterson's book, "Living the Life You Were Meant to Live." It has influenced and helped me in significant ways.

### Finding Your Sweet Spot

I was down by a stream near Winter Park, Colorado, with a group of men. We were talking about calling—about finding your sweet spot and getting in rhythm with what God wants you to do. Sometimes we make it too tough, fighting our way upstream or hacking our own way through the woods. Maybe it is as simple as finding our way into the flow and rhythm of the stream of our life and staying within it.

Remember, this calling thing isn't just about the right job. It's much bigger and deeper than a specific job. Think of a job as an assignment. We may be able to exercise our giftedness and calling in a variety of assignments. Remember that God gives us the passion and energy we need. When the energy, passion and vision are gone, it's time to look for a new assignment. So, as you go through life, make a commitment to do what it takes to stay with the flow or rhythm of your life. Don't get off in those side pools which are stale and stagnant. Not a lot of good comes from stale, standing water. Blow up the obstacles in front of you, change what you need to change to keep moving.

As I look at the way the creek weaves its way down through a valley, it strikes me as true. It takes preparation, patience and intentionality to find the flow and stay in it. But once we are there, just maybe, this path of least resistance is the best place to be! There is a place in the creek where three parts of the creek come together in a sort of "convergence." If we take our life story, our history and experiences and blend them with our talents, strengths and abilities, and then look for opportunities and a context to live out our calling, that may be our sweet spot. Take a journal, head to the river . . . I think God will meet you there!

STOP SIX  -   FINISHING WELL

# FINISHING WELL

*"I have fought the good fight, I have finished the race, I have kept the faith."*
II Timothy 4:7

What marks the people in your life who seem to run this race well? What do the people who live life with a sense of rhythm, balance and purpose have in common? When you think of those who are having a deep impact on others, over the long haul, what comes to mind?

When I think of what it takes to finish, I think about the classic middle school track meet. It often happens like it did in every one of my track meets in middle school. A group of teenage boys approach the start line. Adrenalin is pumping, people are watching, the boys are ready to impress the crowd. The gun fires and the race begins. They only have a few goals at the beginning—start strong, run fast, impress someone. After half a lap, the vast majority of those who burst out of the gate at full speed are now starting to suck wind (that would be me in my brief track career). Early youthful energy always helped me start fast yet fade halfway through the race. At the three-quarter-lap mark they start to fall behind. Those with the most passion and discipline to run the race properly start to take the lead. The ones who pull ahead at the three-quarter-lap mark are the ones who have truly thought about the end result.

Unlike me, our youngest son is a gifted track athlete. He actually was never beat in the hurdles in middle school and ran in the state track meet his freshman year. That is a pretty much polar opposite of my experience. The sprints and the hurdles is where he is at his best. Watching Dylan has convinced me that no matter the distance of the race, the start and how you finish are both critical, but it is not just about those moments. It is about the preparation, training, diet, and rest. It's about harnessing the passion and remembering the reasons you run. It's about adjusting your pace so that you have a reserve of energy left to run a great race, endure and finish strong as well.

So here we are at another check point on our trip together. Any great trip has a beginning, a definitive ending and a lot of great stuff in between, but you must keep your eye on the end of the trip. That is what will help you experience all the things you want to in the short time you have. That is true with a race or a vacation. That is true in a season of life and work, and with relationships as well. You have to sustain a pace and a passion for what you are doing that will not only allow you to keep an eye on the finish line, but to enjoy the journey and finish the race well.

In my family and work, I've tried my best to have the end in mind. The times I failed to do this were the times I put myself, my character, my reputation or my family at risk. I must try to keep my eye on the finish line no matter if I'm facing daily moral or ethical decisions or mundane choices at my workplace. Keeping my eye on the finish line will have a direct, positive impact on my day-to-day decisions. It has to! Looking back to the stories I have shared about family earlier in this book, I wanted to embrace, celebrate and strengthen our kids at significant stages of their lives. Being really serious about that decision had a direct impact on how I spent my time and money throughout the years.

If my desire is to do marriage differently, to stay with my wife for life and do it the right way, then I had better keep my eye on that finish line. Especially considering the temptations and compromising situations that are ready to lure us away on a daily basis.

If my desire is to have my work and leadership values extend beyond myself, then I'd better be about multiplying myself through others and freeing them up to fully utilize their own gifts as well. I'd better resist the temptation to micromanage and seek to empower others to reach for the horizons and chase their dreams.

If I want to have some level of financial independence in the future, then I'd better keep my eye on the end game. If I do, it will have a direct impact on what I spend on a daily and monthly basis. It will cause me to sacrifice something I want, but it will be worth it if I keep a strong awareness of the end game.

If I want to live life with real freedom, consistent and true to the values and convictions God wired in me when He created me, then I'd better know what those are. Then I must step into them with great intentionality, keep an eye on them and surround myself with other people who will hold me accountable to that decision. I'd better have a fierce commitment to do my best to hold to the character it will take to finish life well.

I love what Gordon MacDonald writes about character in his book, "A Resilient Life":

> *"Character is a word that describes the default 'me.' The person I am over the long haul in life. The person who emerges in the most difficult, challenging moments. Character identifies the attitudes, convictions and resulting behaviors that distinguish my life. Let's put it another way: character is what people can expect of me in most situations. Most, I say, because all of us defy or betray our essential character from time to time. When we say 'he acted out of character' we are noting either some exceptionally good or bad behavior that contrasts with what we have come to anticipate of a person. Character, then, is a deep current of what we are day after day after day."[1]*

I love this description for many reasons. One is that finishing well doesn't require that I live under the weight of what others define as proper character. It is not trying to live with other people's convictions. It is not living out of duty and obligation. Finishing well is living consistently with the "attitudes, convictions and resulting behavior that distinguish my life."

That's when we start to be free.

Another reason I like this description is that it doesn't require perfection. Thank God, because I have messed up from time to time. That's not an excuse, it's just real life. I certainly have done some things "out of character" through the years, some things I deeply regret, things I wish I could change. However, through the years, being deeply dependent on God's grace and thankful for His forgiveness, I do believe I have held to the deeper current of who I am and how He has created me.

The Bible is full of examples of people who struggled and violated the deep current of their character from time to time (Peter, Noah, Moses, David, Abraham, just to name a few). What is really amazing to me about these men and their stories is that God continued to pursue them and use them. What was even more outstanding than their accomplishments was how they embraced His grace and forgiveness. When all seemed lost, when many gave up on them, judged or ridiculed them, they shook the dust off their backs and God helped them jump right back in the game. For whatever years I have left on this earth, I want to do the same.

In the church, we are often too ready to cast people off, discount them or throw them aside when there is failure, doubt or struggle. That just is not the picture I see painted again and again in the Bible. I see a God who extends His grace and forgiveness time and time again. I see a God who is about restoration and renewal. At the time of Peter's ultimate failure, his denial of Christ, I see Jesus picking him up, dusting him off and exhorting him to get back in the game. Not only did He want him to get back in the game, but he was going to be the go-to guy . . . the rock. Sure, there was a price to pay and a deep level of brokenness that followed, but through that brokenness, God used him in even deeper ways than ever before. The same can be true with us. When I fall, I desperately need others to help me up, listen, remind me of the truth, and challenge me to get back in the game. I am thankful that I have had others who did just that. Like my friends Tom, Jim, Nate and Dale, who listened, encouraged, prayed and stayed with me at my lowest moments. They were great sounding boards as I emerged from darkness to a place to start dreaming again. I had a few friends who were there with me but, at the same time, they did not let me stay down too long. I don't want to give the enemy an opportunity to totally take me out and, if I stay down too long, that may well happen.

My dad seemed to live with the end in mind. This book is filled with stories about him. He lived a balanced life and his words and actions always seemed to line up. He wasn't close to perfect. No, like all of us, he made his share of mistakes and I'm certain he had a few regrets. I remember one conversation when he openly shared them with me, but he didn't let that hang over his head and bog him down. He kept moving. He didn't get stuck. He didn't let himself be taken out. Relationships were the most important thing to him. His kids never doubted his unconditional love. We knew we were a priority to him. I believe God blessed him in business because he honored God by giving back and doing it the right way. He was a peacemaker, a bridge-builder and a great friend to many. He did not wait until retirement to get time with people or to have fun, which was a good thing since he died so young. He lived out his values and priorities day to day, with frequent stops along the way.

My dad had a great sense of humor. He was a practical joker (no one was safe from his jokes; he could strike at any time). The way he lived life encouraged others to walk with God. His race was way too short, but he ran it well. I have no doubt God welcomed him to heaven with a resounding, "Well done!"

He finished well and left me with a burning desire to do the same. I want the 525,600 minutes I have this year to matter and every year that is to follow. We can finish well, but it will require much from us. It will require planning, passion, perspective, purpose and perseverance.

## Passion

Theodore Wedel wrote a story about a lifesaving station that lost its way and lost its mission. This story has impacted my life in many ways over the years:

> "On a dangerous seacoast where shipwrecks often occur there was once a crude lifesaving station. The building was just a hut, and there was only one boat, but the few devoted members kept a constant watch over the sea, and with no thought for themselves went out day and night tirelessly searching for the lost. Many lives were saved by this wonderful little station, so that it became famous. Some of those who were saved, and various others in the surrounding area, wanted to become associated with the station and give of their time and their money and their effort for the support of its work. New boats were bought and new crews were trained. The little lifesaving station grew.

> "Now some of the members of the lifesaving station became unhappy, in time, however, because the building was so crude and so poorly equipped. They felt that a more comfortable, suitable place should be provided as the first refuge for those saved from the sea. And so they replaced the emergency cots with beds, and they put better furniture in the now enlarged building, so that now the lifesaving station actually became a popular gathering place for its members. They took great care in decorating it beautifully and furnishing it exquisitely, for they found

*new uses for it in the context of a sort of club. But fewer members were now interested in going to sea on lifesaving missions, and so they hired lifesaving crews to do this work on their behalf, and in their stead. Now, don't misunderstand, the lifesaving motif still prevailed in the club's decoration and symbols – there was a liturgical lifeboat (symbolic rather than fully functional) in the room where the club initiations were held, for example – so the changes did not necessarily mean that the original purposes were totally lost.*

*"About this time a large ship was wrecked off the coast, and the hired crews brought in boatloads of cold and wet, half-drowned people. They were dirty people and they were sick people, some of them had black skin, some with yellow skin. The beautiful new club, as you might imagine, was thrown into chaos, so that the property committee immediately had a shower house built outside the club where these recent victims of shipwreck could be cleaned up before coming inside the main clubhouse.*

*"At the very next meeting, there was a split in the club membership. Most of the members wanted to stop the club's lifesaving activities for being so unpleasant, as well as for being a hindrance to the normal social life of the club. Some members insisted upon lifesaving as their primary purpose, pointing out that, indeed, they were still called a lifesaving station. But these few were finally voted down and told that if they wanted to save the lives of all the various kinds of people who were shipwrecked in those waters, they could begin their own lifesaving station down the coast. And so, they did just that.*

*"Now as the years passed, the new station down the coast came to experience the very same changes that had occurred in the older, initial station. It evolved into a club, and yet another lifesaving station had to be founded to restore the original purpose.*

*"Well, history continued to repeat itself, so that if you visit that seacoast today, you will find a great number of exclusive clubs along*

*that shore. Shipwrecks are frequent in those waters, but most of the people drown!"*[2]

Having a crystal clear mission is an important lesson of this story. But, the question I've often asked is this — what compels a person to get in the boat day after day? On those cold stormy mornings and dark damp nights, what would keep pushing you to get in the lifesaving boats and head out to sea? Passion is what it takes — passion for the mission, a passion that won't let you rest, a passion that compels you to get back in the boat, no matter the obstacles that are in your way.

Passion is what keeps you going. In the movie, "The Perfect Storm,"[3] there is a great scene where the Coast Guard pilots jump out of their helicopter into pitch black darkness and 40-foot waves on the edge of a hurricane to rescue three people below. Why would they do that? How could they possibly ready themselves for that moment? They were able to do it because they could always answer the question, "Why?" They were passionately committed and focused to a compelling mission.

Are you passionate about work and the journey you are on? Don't get too comfortable. Being comfortable and safe can be a great enemy of passion. It can dull it or eliminate it all together. In fact, here are some key enemies of passion: familiarity, boredom, routine and repetition. There is a need and reality to certain routines and predictability in our lives. Nevertheless, let's face it—in relationships, if it comes down to routines and lists and only what's familiar or certain, we are at risk of losing our passion. In fact, we could lose the best part of the relationship as well. We may even lose the relationship altogether.

Psalms 51:10–13 is probably my favorite passage in the Bible. "Create in me a pure heart, O God, and renew a steadfast spirit within me. Do not cast me from your presence or take your Holy Spirit from me. Restore to me the joy of your salvation and grant me a willing spirit, to sustain me. Then I will teach transgressors your ways, and sinners will turn back to you."

There are some key indicators in these verses that will help us live a life of significance and impact: a clean heart, steadfast spirit, a commitment to restore the joy of our salvation and a deep desire for a willing spirit. If we desire these things and take steps toward them, I believe good things will happen.

Renew, sustain and restore the joy. What does it mean to restore the joy of your salvation? It means you have to remember. Like I talked about earlier, you have got to remember those key God moments. Remember the times God changed you and others in your life. Remember the desperate need you and others have had for Jesus. Hold on to those times. That is what will help you connect to your passion. That is what will get you back into that boat, day after day.

Keep your focus clear, have some preset boundaries, stay in the company of a few and remind yourself often of why you do what you do. Make sure you leave the safety of your current circumstance to discover, explore new ideas and dream.

**Perspective**

For several years, I taught a seminar for parents of teens. When I first started teaching that seminar, one of the things that made me so good was that I didn't have any teens myself! I soon realized the answers were not so easy. In fact, things could get pretty messy. Through the years, the message of the seminar became more simple: be clear, pursue relationships wirh your kids and fight to keep a good perspective.

It may not "feel" like what we're doing is making a difference, but I believe if we relentlessly pursue a relationship with our kids, it will make a difference. Sooner or later, it will make a difference. When I was preparing for one of the talks, I stumbled across a letter in the newspaper written from one father to another. In essence, it talked about a son's view of his father at different ages:

*"Age 4 - My dad can do anything.*

*Age 7 - Dad knows a lot, a whole lot.*

*Age 8 - Father doesn't know quite everything.*

*Age 14 - Father is hopelessly old-fashioned.*

*Age 21 - Oh, that man is out of date . . . what did you expect?*

*Age 25 - He knows a little about it but not much.*

*Age 30 - Maybe we ought to find out what Dad thinks.*

*Age 35 - A little patience; let's get Dad's assessment before we do anything.*

*Age 50 - I wonder what Dad would have thought about that, he was pretty smart.*

*Age 60 - Dad, he knew literally everything.*

*Age 65 - I would give anything if Dad were here, I really miss that man."*[4]

For me, losing my dad in my 20s gave me a quick perspective. Over the last 20 years, many times I found myself aching for conversation with him. Many days I find myself saying, "I would give anything if Dad were here, I really miss that man."

It's a great reminder of the importance of perspective, not only in parenting, but in the broader context of life. It helps to understand where others are on the journey and how it will impact us.

In terms of a relationship with God, perspective says everything has a season. There will be times of growth and bearing fruit, and times of dormancy, and all of it is okay. There will be times in our lives when we will "feel" really close to God. We will be eager to grow and learn and worship. There will be times when we'll have lots of opportunities to share with others and then, there will be times when we feel like we're in a desert. We will ask all kinds of questions during those dormant times. Why is God allowing this to happen? Is God even real or is this all just a setup for disappointment? Why does He seem to be silent? Is this pursuit of God really worth it? Will it ever really make a difference? Does He care about the little things of my life? Is He with me even if it doesn't feel like it? Keep asking the questions. Don't be afraid to struggle. Be honest with God and others. Most of all, hang on during those desert times. Those are great times to wait, listen and be quiet. Don't give up. Don't force things. If your time in the wilderness stretches on for weeks, months or even years, stay strong and hang on! He will break through to you. You may need something that you can only get in the desert.

Moses, a man very familiar with desert times, asked God for a sense of perspective, to teach him to number his days. It is never too early, or too late, to begin praying this prayer. We are never too young to start thinking about what we will leave behind. This is what I tried to communicate to our son when I wrote to him on the night of his high school graduation:

*Journal Entry, June 2, 2006*

*It's a common thing for kids to say, "Life is short so make it a party." No doubt God wants us to have fun and enjoy life to its fullest. I think I have modeled that for you very well. But the key is to be intentional and balanced, because time does go so quickly.*

*So many people waste months and years away with a superficial lifestyle that has no plan, direction, focus or purpose. Don't make that mistake. Life really is too short. Yesterday, a 19-year-old girl you knew died . . . I know she thought she still had forever.*

*For all of us, the lesson is to live life not by accident, but with purpose every day.*

*Have fun, study and work hard, invest deeply in the right people, seize every moment to share with others about your relationship with God. Live life differently than other people. Find ways to invest in people's lives in ways that last, help connect people together, laugh as much as you can, find things that you really enjoy and go do them. Force yourself to get alone to think, listen and pray and write things down. That always helps me make the most of the days in front of me. Remember to put relationships first. Life's too short to let petty disagreements, rules, lists, etc. come between us and people who are really important.*

There is a scene in the movie "Dead Poets Society" where the teacher takes his young students to the school's trophy case. He has them stare into photos of the young men and look at the lists of their accomplishments.

*"They're not that different from you, are they? Same haircuts. Full of hormones, just like you. Invincible, just like you feel. The world is their oyster. They believe they're destined for great things, just like many of you, their eyes are full of hope, just like you. Did they wait until it was too late to make from their lives even one iota of what they were capable? Because, you see gentlemen, these boys are now fertilizing daffodils. But if you listen real close, you can hear them whisper their legacy to you. Go on, lean in. Listen, you hear it? —Carpe—hear it? — Carpe, carpe diem, seize the day boys, make your lives extraordinary."[5]*

John Keating was giving his students perspective. He challenged them to discover what their dreams are, then chase them with all their heart, to live each day like it was their last—not with a reckless attitude, but rather with a sense of purpose and hope. This is a critical message for any student at any age.

## Purpose

Purpose and hope are what keep us moving ahead in life. As we talked about earlier in this book, we need to have some overarching purposes in our life, callings that we pursue throughout our days, but we also need to have short-term goals that spur us on.

Somewhere I read a story about greyhound dogs that were used for racing. To get these dogs to run fast, trainers release a mechanical rabbit that runs around the track. One day, the rabbit broke down and the dogs stopped running. They didn't know what to do. They needed a new goal to chase in order to keep going.

The key to continually moving ahead seems to be to start something new before you bottom out where you are. That could take two years or 20 years, it doesn't really matter. What does matter, though, is being brutally honest with yourself. Do you still have passion and vision for what you're doing? Are you being faithful to the deeper current of who you are? As a leader, do others have more ideas, more vision than you do? Are you emotionally "tapped out"? Be alert to indicators that may signal that it's time to move on to a new goal. Don't stay too long, don't leave too early.

After 25 years with Youth for Christ/Campus Life, I transitioned to a new job and ministry. God was calling me to something new, but it was critical for me that before I transitioned, I had to finish well. That meant a lot of different things. It meant building great teams and releasing them to do ministry. It meant building others up and preparing them for leadership. It meant letting others get the spotlight and releasing control of some things. It meant keeping others focused on the vision and keeping the main thing the main thing. It meant moving to a point of personal surrender and a continual personal pursuit of God. It meant knowing all the loose ends could not be tied up. It meant releasing control and trusting others. It meant giving it my best all the way through and continually multiplying myself through others the best I could. It meant leaving this ministry in good standing financially, relationally and otherwise and, at some point, it meant that I did actually have to finish. I had to have the guts to step away.

What does it mean for you to finish well? It means you embrace each season of life with passion and fervor. It means you take hold of the responsibilities and relationships that God has placed in your life and continue to invest and pour into those until He tells you otherwise. Decide what all this means for you and then set a course to finish strong. Some people go through life moving from one thing to another with no sense of mission and no grasp on what it means to finish. The result can be a wake of mediocrity that they leave behind. Don't be one of those people that cuts and runs; be a finisher! That doesn't mean you have to stay somewhere 20 years. There is no timeline attached here. That's up to you and God, and yes, you may be uniquely gifted as a starter, a developer or a maintainer. You might be one who starts, multiplies and moves to the next thing, but I do believe we are all called to finish well, no matter what our gift mix. In a relationship, on the job, with a neighbor or in a particular season of life, what does it mean for you to not just hang in there and keep the status quo, but what would it mean to finish well?

## Perseverance

Finishing well also requires perseverance. My mom showed me what this looks like. She was still in her early 60s, but a second run of cancer had really taken its toll. This time it was in her brain and spinal fluid and she was in a long-term care facility. Throughout her life she reached out to others, served them, loved them and shared the gospel with them. Her last days were no different.

She was reaching out to others right up to her last days on earth. She often asked the nurses around her if they knew for sure they would see her in heaven. She talked the Christian talk, she walked the walk and she loved other people on good days and bad. We went to see her one Labor Day weekend, only weeks before she died. She had a hard time standing and a harder time staying focused as her brain cancer was in full force. Nevertheless, as soon as we got there, she went to the kitchen, and with one hand on the counter to steady herself, she made our kids a malt and some lunch. She served them until her last days. She reached out to others, sharing with them the hope of a relationship with God, even when it was difficult. She was used by God in the best of times and the worst of times. She modeled for me what it meant to persevere and finish well.

I am fortunate enough to have a rich spiritual heritage—grandparents who were pioneers, who built a financial and spiritual foundation for their family and future generations; a mother who loved people deeply and served relentlessly, even in her darkest days; a father who never met my children but passed on to me a balanced life, a love for family and an authentic walk with God. They were far from perfect. They had many struggles, but the foundation was built strong to sustain any harsh weather that threatened their faith.

Both of my grandmothers read thier Bibles and had their devotions to their last days on this earth. One said the Lord's Prayer every day; the other was more spontaneous with her prayers. One memorized a Bible verse every week, well into her 80s. One was very structured in her pursuit of God, the other was more spontaneous in her expression of worship and faith.

One grandfather was a risk-taker, a pioneer, a builder who flourished through the Great Depression. The other was a faithful provider who worked his last days at the Phillips 66 gas station. All of them endured much, worked hard, laughed frequently, struggled through deep hardship, valued family and walked with God as best they could. In their own way, they all finished well.

I also think of my aunt. She grew up on our family farm in Kenesaw, Nebraska. She pulled horses through the fields and raised livestock. During the Great Depression, she got a degree and began to teach school. She helped pay for some of the family vacation trips I wrote about earlier. After she got married, she and her husband ran a hunting / fishing camp in the backwoods of Maine.

One winter, she had to snowshoe several miles out of camp with their young son on her back to get him to the hospital. Years later, she received a Master's Degree and once again taught school for many years. After her husband died, she moved back to Nebraska to be close to my dad and to be part of our family. Many years later, she was reacquainted with a man she knew 50 years earlier. They were married in thier 80s and started another great adventure.

She lived life to the fullest. She experienced much. I remember her for her servant's attitude, love of music and willingness to take risks. My children remember her for cooking them fresh lobster and homemade bread.

She stayed in a relationship with God her whole life. She struggled at times, experiencing failure and wrestling with weaknesses and sin, like many of us do, but she kept walking with God throughout her whole life. She seldom wavered. She kept learning. She played music until she physically couldn't do it anymore. She deeply valued family and she generally held to the deeper current of who she was—she finished well.

So, how about you? What marks the people in your life who are running this race well? When I think of all these people in my own life, the common trait that often comes to mind is a relentless pursuit of Jesus. They were people who believed that, not only was a real, authentic encounter with Jesus possible, but it was life changing and they were relentless in their pursuit of Him! They seemed willing to create the space and have a pace to their lives that would allow that to happen.

When I think about this, my mind is drawn to those out-of-control guys in Mark 2. You know the story. These guys were desperate to have their hurting friend encounter Jesus. They were crazy enough to believe that, if they could just get their friend to be at Jesus' feet, it would be life changing. They were so committed to that pursuit that they vowed to do whatever it took to make that happen.

So they did.

They fought the crowds, climbed onto the roof, cut a hole in it and lowered him down. It's hard to imagine that scene, maybe a little bit like the push I felt in the 12th row of a Coldplay concert. Whatever it was like, we know that it was life-altering to their friend because he was healed. I suspect it was equally impacting to those risk-taking dreamers as well. Guys who probably had a plan and then were willing to change that plan, but stayed committed to pursuing Jesus, no matter what!

So, what does that look like for you? What would you need to do, change or adjust to keep pursuing that encounter with Christ? For me, I know the first step is asking myself if I really believe in my heart that an encounter with Jesus is possible. Then, do I expect it to be life-changing, on a day-to-day, hour-by-hour basis? Once I am honest with myself on that, then the stage is set. I can unplug and create the pace in my life that will allow it to happen.

## An Eye on the Finish Line

No matter where you're at today, no matter what your struggles have been, no matter whether you have fallen or not, no matter what your personal or family history has been, you can still finish strong. As I shared earlier, despite the legacy I was given, I came to points in my life of real difficulty and struggle. I could have taken a path out of pride, independence, boredom, disappointment or outright rebellion and my life could have gone down an entirely different road. By God's grace and because of a faithful few, an incredible wife and God's relentless pursuit of me, that did not happen. So, it really does come down to you. With the hand you've been dealt, what will you do? There is an important factor here—what you do now will have an impact on how you finish. How you respond to failure, success, struggle and disappointment will also affect the finish.

For most of his life, my wife's father was a bitter, cynical man. He rejected his daughter by not investing any time in her. He was angry at his family, at politicians, at the church and at God. Like all of us, he had a story — a story that gave great insight into who he was. He was a hard man, but had a life marred by service in World War II and by the loss of a son. Fourteen months before he died, he began to search and struggle with the emptiness he felt. Despite the years of hurt, Marcia never gave up on him. She prayed for him and stuck with him. In the last months of his life, he met Christ and began to grow in his relationship with God. Some of the hurt within Marcia was healed. He died soon after he began his walk with God and he finished well.

Life tosses many ups and downs our way. There are exciting times and times of deep disappointment. As you walk through it, you have to remember that you are not alone. Do you believe that? Do I really believe that? As I hit the stretch run of writing this book, my faith journey took a serious hit. After the events of the last few weeks, my walk of faith looks and feels a lot different. With someone so close to me encountering such pain, I wonder if God really is with us, and I want to know if He really is involved with our daily lives? Do I really believe He is good? Or is it just empty words? What does it look like for me to trust God today?

I was sitting on the boardwalk in Mission Beach, California, desperately needing to be alone and find some peace amidst the storm in my soul. I wanted to hear something, anything from God. I was wondering if I really had anything to offer the young leaders that were coming into The Harbor ministry events we were launching. What would I tell them about this faith journey today? So there I sat, the colors over the ocean were awesome, and the waves seemed to bring the first moments of peace that I had felt in days. As I listened to my favorite Sigur Ros song, I sensed a deepening connection with all that was going on around me when he approached. I did not know him, I did not want to talk to him, but he quietly approached, ignored my nasty looks, and asked me if I ever had been in such a peaceful place. With great emotion, tears in his eyes and strength in his voice, he told me that he was overwhelmed by the peace of God at that moment. He reached for my hand, and said "God bless you" and he was gone. Suddenly I was in a very deep place.

Somehow, through all the fog, confusion and pain, God sent me a messenger. Someone to remind me that you can find peace in the storm. There are seasons and moments that God breaks through. I don't understand how it all fits together. Why does He seem to show up so unassuming, so subtle, yet so powerfully at times? Yet at other times He seems so quiet, so absent, so uninvolved. I don't know why that is, but for a brief moment with an ocean, a song and a stranger, I had an encounter with the Creator and it left me longing for more. I left that moment with a deeper sense that God is with us in all that life throws our way, in the joy, the pain, the aloneness, the wandering, the discoveries. I believe He grieves with us, laughs with us and experiences life with us all the way through. He is with us now and He will be there when we reach the end of this leg of our journey.

A critical part of finishing well is deciding that you will take the next step of faith and never give up on God, because He certainly will not give up on you. I also need to remind myself often that it's not about performance — the lists, the dos and don'ts. It's all about relationships. The writings of author John Eldredge have impacted me deeply the last few years. He often talks about following God, not out of a sense of duty and obligation, but out of grace, desire and freedom. Some who don't finish well in the journey often falter here. I believe He doesn't care about lists and He's not keeping an account of our failures, no matter how bad we think they are. The enemy wants to bury us in guilt and regret and give us a hopeless feeling that we will never get it right, but God sustains and inspires us, embraces us and keeps us moving toward Him.

He wants us to be free.

He's not concerned with what we can do for Him; He just wants us to pursue Him. It's not about the seven things we must do to stay the course. We have a God who wants a relationship with us. Many who don't finish well miss the simplicity of God's grace. They miss the simple fact that it's not about what we can do. It's not about duty, tasks, principles or steps to anything. It's about relationship. We cannot let past successes or past failures, indifference, apathy or disappointment take us out. The main thing is to be relentless in your pursuit.

Finishing well is not about avoiding hardships, staying safely in the harbor and never venturing out to the open seas. It's not about settling for the easy route—it's going right through the deep waters.

I think finishing well is all about risk, choices, chance, faith, unpredictability and the experience of new things.

*"When we walk to the edge of all the light we have and take the step into the darkness of the unknown, we must believe that one of two things*

*will happen. There will be something solid for us to stand on or we will be taught to fly."*[6]

It's about knowing that, when you come right up to the edge, you are not alone and it is at that edge that the adventure and discovery begins. It's about choosing well among all the millions of options this world has to offer us. We have more choices today than any other generation in the history of the world. Finishing well is about discernment; it's about having a natural walk with God in a deep enough way that you can trust your instincts and intuition on a daily basis.

For me, it is all of that. It's about a life of faith, not fear. It's about accepting God's forgiveness. It's about staying deeply connected to others, remembering that, no matter what your past has been about, God wants a relationship with you and wants you to live a life of deep impact. It's about staying humble and knowing that God has allowed you be successful for a reason. It's about loyalty and faithfulness to people, even when you feel they don't deserve it. It's about longevity and staying-power despite the detours and wrecks that life sometimes throws at us.

Finishing well is about finding what things are life-giving to us and not life-quenching. So, like we talked about earlier, what brings you life and what sucks the life right out of you? God made us with interests, passions, strengths and abilities and a heart that comes alive in certain situations. Listen to that, look for it, embrace it, because those things will not only help you live longer, they will also help you finish well.

*Hebrews 12:1–3. "Therefore, since we are surrounded by such a great cloud of witnesses, let us throw off everything that hinders and the sin that so easily entangles, and let us run with perseverance the race marked out for us. Let us fix our eyes on Jesus, the author and perfecter of faith, who for the joy set before him endured the cross, scorning its shame, and sat down at the right hand of the throne of God. Consider him who endured such opposition from sinful men, so that you will not grow weary and lose heart."*

Cast off everything that will hinder you. Spend some time here. Is there anything you're holding onto that will weigh you down, slow you down and eventually prohibit you from finishing well? Be honest with yourself, ask others to speak into this for you. Is there anything you need to cast off? Or at this point, is there anything you need to change or adjust? Again, be honest, are you currently on a pace that you can sustain? Don't rush this. Take a few hours and seek God on this. One way or another, He will bring things to mind. Once you've dealt with that, keep a tenacious eye on a relationship with Jesus, remember those key "God" moments. Do not forget them, hang on to those times. That's what will get you through.

Decide now that you will be more than a starter, more than a wanderer on a journey. Whatever it means in specific areas of your life, make a commitment today that, in your family, work, ministry and friendships, you will do what it takes, day after day after day, so that you can finish well.

STOP SEVEN  -  THE STORY YOU LEAVE BEHIND

# THE STORY YOU LEAVE BEHIND

*"The leader of the band is tired and his eyes are growing old.*
*But his blood runs through my instrument*
*And his song is in my soul.*
*My life has been a poor attempt to imitate the man.*
*I'm just a living legacy to the leader of the band."*[1]

*-Excerpts from "Leader of the Band," by Dan Fogelberg*

I do have a confession to make: as a younger person, I was a notorious scrapbooker but, I want to make it clear, I don't scrapbook now. I don't host scrapbook parties. I don't invite people over to sell those expensive scrapbooking kits.

However, when I was young, I kept track of everything. Even though I was the youngest, I was the one who kept the pictures and wrote down the key memories after a family vacation. I was the one who wanted to preserve the memory of that trip and make sure no one forgot that special event. That particular hobby continued in different ways as I got older. Most of the time I would organize the trips and experiences that would bring people together. In many ways, even though the faces and places are different, I still do this today. It's a great window into who I was, what I valued as a young person and what I still value today. It gives some insight into my calling now. It is part of a legacy I will surely leave others.

We all leave a mark—a legacy that lingers long after we are gone, whether it is intentional or accidental, intensely positive or negative. We will be remembered for something.

So what comes to mind as you think about the people who have left a mark on your life? Think back, way back, to a few people who marked your journey in a positive way. Write those thoughts down, don't lose the lessons of the road.

If you are at all skeptical about the deep impact you can have on others, think about this. Were you ever involved in athletics? Ponder some of your past coaches for a moment. If there is any doubt about the impact we can have on others with our words, values, and day to day interactions, this should clear that up. Did you have a coach that believed in you no matter what? A coach at any level can have a powerful impact in the lives of people with both words and actions.

I've played for coaches that have instilled fear and rattled my confidence. And, I've played for those who inspired me and believed in me no matter the circumstances. They challenged me to not be content with ordinary, but to push myself to be the best. After all these years, both have left a mark.

Whether in short-term or long-term relationships, in our work or our connections to those around us, we will all leave a mark. It is what the next generations may know and remember about us. Our legacy might be something tangible like the cabin my dad built. It might be something less tangible like the stories, impressions, values and memories that surround each of our lives.

My dad's friend, George Osborne, said that my dad was the only one who could make him slow down and step out of his Type A attitude. "With Lloyd, things were in balance. You could throw away the clocks, watches and agendas and just enjoy life and friendships. Here it is, over 20 years after he died, and he has still left his mark deeply in my life." Now, that's a legacy!

Over 40 years ago, my cousins spent their summers on our family farm. One still tells stories of my dad's deep impact on his life, an impact that has lasted to this day! When I remember stories like those, I want to step it up! I want to leave a mark that causes people to pause and want to be "more," simply because of what they have seen in my life. There have been times when I felt like I've made a decision that would threaten the legacy I want to leave. However, God has shown me that how I respond after failure and success can be equally important and, as I shared earlier, even though there will be times of struggle and failure, there will also be times of grace, faithfullness and forgiveness. The pressure is off, I don't have to be perfect to leave a great legacy. There is no how-to manual for it, but I do need to fight for and hang on to the deep current of who I am and what I was created to be, day after day after day.

In part, my life will be shaped by the impact of my parents and the impact of others on my life. But mostly it is up to me and it's up to you to steward the passions, talents and burdens that are uniquely yours.

My father was a builder and I am a fisherman. When he was building that family cabin in the winter of 1971, I tried to be like him. I would start the day determined to build, but the lake was irresistible. I wanted to fish; building was not in my DNA. My dad understood. He didn't insist that I needed to be a builder. He let me take my fishing pole and spend hours chasing the bass and crappie. I vividly remember the scene of me sitting by the lake, pulling in fish and hearing the sounds of him building his dream. While he was building, he gave me the freedom to be a fisherman.

In many ways, in my relationships and in my work, I've been that fisherman, seeking to catch the elusive hearts of people and turn them toward something bigger than themselves. I strive to bring people together for shared life experiences and in my life story, I have been pretty relentless in my pursuit of meaning, significance and a bigger story. I hope my life has shown a deep desire to come alongside many others on their journey, to encourage and hopefully inspire others to keep chasing God and the dreams He has given them. I hope this is part of my legacy.

As a fisherman, I knew it was okay to enjoy life, to listen to my heart. I knew I must be patient and get myself quiet so I could hear the still small voice of God and I knew I had to be as creative, intuitive and passionate about the process as I was about the results.

Dad, the builder, always seemed to have a plan, but was also ready to scrap the plan for a better one. He seemed to always be on purpose, content with time and process; he often had his eyes on the finish line.

I learned many great lessons from the builder:

God uniquely gifted me

Understand and embrace my strengths, talents, values and convictions

Remember that it is as much about the process as it is the outcome

I'm free to be who God created me to be

Work hard and finish what I start

Play hard, laugh, have fun

Don't get rattled by circumstances I can't control

Honor God by taking steps toward my dreams

Don't let the world, or others define me

Be willing to step out and take risks

When I mess up, embrace God's incredible grace and forgiveness and get back in the game

Keep moving, don't get stuck

I hope that I am able to fish as effectively as my dad was able to build and, when I'm gone, that my legacy will be as powerful and as positive as his.

I think it's wise to stop one more time and ask ourselves some key questions about what we are leaving in our wake and what will continue to cause ripples or waves after we're gone.

If you were to live the next years with the mindset of leaving a legacy, how would you want to be remembered? How do you want your family, friends, co-workers and others in your sphere of influence to think of you when you're gone?

If you knew that your headstone would be written at the end of next year, what would you want it to say and how would you live from here on out in order to shape a legacy one year at a time?

For me, I want to be remembered as a man who had fun on this journey. Someone who created memories, persevered, loved his family, showed grace to others, impacted people and pursued God on the mountaintops and in the valleys. I want to be thought of as someone who, despite mistakes and shortcomings, stayed in the race, enjoyed each leg of that race, took risks, learned from my failures and kicked it in to finish strong in each stage of the journey. Most importantly, I want to be passionate about embracing and pursuing the mystery of God, resolute not to box God into some predetermined shape or view, never so arrogant to think I have Him figured out. I want to stay authentically connected to the deep current of who I am and who God created me to be throughout my life. Lastly, I want to be a companion for many on this journey.

When I think of you, as you read this book, I want you to know that a life of faith can bring great joy and peace, even in times of deep sorrow and pain, even in times of great chaos, and heartbreak. I want you to know that you, too, can have a life of deep impact. I want you to remember that everyone leaves a mark, everyone leaves a legacy. You can choose what your legacy will be. I hope you live life with a deep sense of mission and passion that is based on an understanding of your own unique calling. I want you to seize the day and enjoy the journey because every day is a great gift. I challenge you to commit to regular times to come into the "harbor" to seek silence, solitude and rest; to get the resources, the encouragement and the inspiration you need for the next stage of the journey. I want you to cling to key God moments and write them down, remembering the times He has uniquely met you. This will help give strength for the journey.

So, what will it be for you? Are you ready to live with intentionality and strength? Are you ready to take the next step in your journey to keep moving, to avoid getting stagnant and stuck by the struggles, failure and the obstacles that lie ahead? Are you determined not to let the views of others or their limited views of God determine who you will be and how you will live out your faith? Even if you are young, do you know what you want your life to be about? Do you have a sense for the "mark" you will leave and want to leave with others?

I want to end this book with some words I passed on to my son as he headed off to college. My great hope is that, no matter your age, it will encourage and inspire you to take the next steps in your journey.

**Legacy**

*Journal Entry, September 05, 2006*

*So here it is, the last moment in this journal. It's weird, I don't want to finish it because I know it represents to me the ending of this chapter of life, but I also know that it doesn't matter whether I'm ready for it or not, this season is ending and a new season of life is about to begin.*

*I've tried my best to be authentic and real with the words in this journal. I haven't always done it right but I believe, to the best of my ability, there has been alignment with my words and my actions. Having that integrity is critical. I've tried over the years not only to say these things to you, but I've tried to model them and live them in such a way that you can see them in me. I'm not saying I've always done it right because I haven't, and there are some things I would certainly change. There have been times I was out of alignment, but God didn't give up on me and He will never give up on you either. Everybody is wired differently. For me, I remember many times in my younger years being excited to be a dad. Something in me longed for that role.*

*After my dad died just before you were born, I committed whole-heartedly to the role of being a father, to seize every moment possible and, to the best of my ability, to go through those initial years of being a dad with no regrets.*

*Of course, there are things I would change and do differently but, for the most part, I wanted to put relationships first and I think I have done that. Hopefully, in many ways, I showed you guys that you were a clear priority. For the most part, I've gone through these first 19 years of your life with no regrets in my relationship with you and I hope that will continue for as long as God gives us.*

*I have deeply enjoyed and will continue to enjoy investing in your life. It has been a blast to think of ways to create lasting memories. The experience I would never trade and I'm looking forward to the years ahead. At the same time I know it will be different.*

*Last spring I was able to see Aunt Dee one more time before she went to heaven. She was in the middle of literally writing her life story. Many times over the last few years, I would encourage her to keep writing and keep remembering. She was the last one of her generation and there was much we all could learn from her and her experiences. I would give questions to her to think about and we had many great discussions as she recalled her parents (your great-grandparents) living out their faith in God through a variety of different circumstances. Every time I was with her, I would encourage her to keep writing. She never quite finished her project and, the last morning I was with her, she knew she couldn't do any more. Actually, her last words to me were, "Tim, you're going to have to finish the story..."*

*Maybe that's what these long journals are partly about; my desire to keep it going and now that's really where you and I are in this journey. I'll keep investing in you and others, but you are at the stage of life to carry it out and write some new chapters in this great legacy that others have left for us.*

*So pick up your pack and hit the road. I'm going to love to see and "read" your entries in this journal of your life and know I'm really proud of you! 1 Timothy 4:12 says let no one look down on your youthfulness but through speech, conduct, love, faith and purity, make yourself an example to others, and Proverbs 3:5-6 says to keep your focus on God and He will make your paths straight.*

*So go for it! Chase those dreams! Stay the course.*

*Remember; it's your time to write the story.*

The same is true for you. Your mistakes are in the past. God's forgiveness and restoration are complete and immediate. He aches for you to step into all that He wants for you. No matter what your life circumstances, the time ahead of you is a great gift. How will you use it? In the journey of your life, it's your time . . . your time to write the story.

**REMEMBER, IT'S YOUR TIME TO WRITE THE STORY**

## STOP ONE  -  FIND THE RHYTHM

1. To Sir, With Love, Director, James Clevell, Columbia Pictures, Culver City, CA, 1967.

## STOP TWO  -  KNOW THE HORIZON

1. Tom Petty, "Time to Move On," from the album Wildflowers, Warner Brothers, Burbank, CA, 1994.

2. City Slickers, Director, Ron Underwood, Columbia Pictures, Culver City, CA, 1991.

3. Michele Chrisp, taken from unpublished writing.

4. Ron Jensen, Achieving Authentic Success (Temecula, CA: Future Achievement International, 2002).

## STOP THREE  -  DON'T DO THIS ALONE

1. John Eldredge, Waking the Dead (Nashville, TN: Thomas Nelson, Inc., 2003), 187-188.

2. Green Day, "Boulevard of Broken Dreams," from the album American Idiot, Reprise, Burbank, CA, 2004.

## STOP FOUR  -  REMEMBER THOSE NEAR

1. Father Facts ®, Fifth Edition (Gaithersburg, MD, National Fatherhood Initiative 2007) 20, 23, 123-135.

2. Remember the Titans, Director, Boaz Yakin, Buena Vista Pictures, Burbank, CA, 2000.

3. Robert Lewis, Raising a Modern-Day Knight (Carol Stream, IL: Tyndale House Publishers, Inc., 1997).

## STOP FIVE - EMBRACE THE MYSTERY

1. Webster's New Collegiate Dictionary (Springfield, MA: G & C Merriam Company, 1974), 158.

2. Ken Gire, Windows of the Soul (Grand Rapids, MI: Zondervan, 1996).

3. The Breakfast Club, Director, John Hughes, Universal Studios, Universal City, CA, 1985.

4. Oswald Chambers, My Utmost for His Highest, Oswald Chambers Publications Association, 1963

## STOP SIX - FINISHING WELL

1. Gordon MacDonald, A Resilient Life, (Nashville, TN: Thomas Nelson, Inc., 2004), 62-63.

2. Theodore Wedel, "A Crude Lifesaving Station," from the following web site http://www.resurrection.org/crude_lifesaving_station.htm.

3. The Perfect Storm, Director, Wolfgang Petersen, Burbank, CA, Warner Brothers, 2000.

4. Danbury, Conn New - Times

5. Dead Poets Society, Director, Peter Weir, Burbank, CA, Touchstone Pictures, 1989.

6. Frank Outlaw, "Edges," from the following web site http://randomquotes.org/quote/16189-when-we-walk-to-the-edge-of-all-the-light-we-have-.html.

## STOP SEVEN - THE STORY YOU LEAVE BEHIND

1. Dan Fogelberg, "Leader of the Band," from the album The Innocent Age, Full Moon Records, location unknown, 1981.

WWW.HARBORSEVEN.COM

21725495R00085

Made in the USA
San Bernardino, CA
02 June 2015